presentationsin

The Practical Guide to Stop Offending (and Start Impressing) Your Audience

ALAN HOFFLER

WORDS OF PRAISE

"There are those who are excellent performers, from athletics to science to public speaking. There are those who are gifted at teaching people to be excellent performers. Then there is the rare person who is gifted at doing as well as teaching. There is no better speaker or speaker's coach than Alan Hoffler. He will compassionately tell you what you need to hear, has immense patience for those who truly desire to maximize their talent, and has the ability to help you improve faster than you can believe possible.

Oie Osterkamp
Executive director, Ronald McDonald House of Durham

"I credit Alan Hoffler with helping me go from good to great as a speaker. His process was easy to understand and I could see my improvement immediately. I now know what to focus on and what to S.T.O.P. doing in order to become a more effective communicator."

Stan Phelps
Founder, 9 INCH marketing
Author of *Purple Goldfish, Green Goldfish*, and *Golden Goldfish*

Alan Hoffler is not only a master communicator, he's also a masterful coach and trainer. His expertise is tremendously valuable, and he makes the process of working with him a great joy. When we first started working together my presentations lacked structure and weren't as engaging as I'd like. After taking Alan's classes and hiring him to work with me one on one, I walked away with a reusable strategy to create amazing presentations. I now have greater confidence in knowing that I'm serving my audience at a much higher level, and I'm excited to share that my results validate it!

Melissa West (Malueg)
President of Xtreme Results, LLC

"Eighteen years in public education made me confident connecting with people in front of a room. Seven years facilitating workshops in corporate settings made me feel like a content expert. But it wasn't until I spent two days in Alan Hoffler's Powerful, Persuasive Speaking workshop that I believed I could be a virtuoso presenter. Alan broke down the presentation process into its key components; shone a gentle and clear light on my ineffective practices; and coached me to deliver like a maestro. I was genuinely amazed at how much, and how quickly, I grew. Best of all, the lessons I learned from Alan carry their power into many other relationships and forms of communication. I'm not just a better presenter; I'm a better person."

Bob Stocking
Master instructor, Vervago, Inc.

"With no hyperbole, Alan Hoffler has changed my life. Alan doesn't merely teach the communication 'tactics' necessary to increase the bottom line of your business or to persuade people to your particular point of view, although these are both likely byproducts of putting into practice what he imparts. Alan imparts something much more valuable, however—an increased potential to leave the legacy you desire to leave. I will be forever grateful for the gift he has given me."

Wes Simmons
Co-owner, Dynamite Sports, Inc.
Co-owner, 3D Institute, LLC

"I love Alan's approach to coaching! I have taken giant steps forward in my ability to engage a crowd by putting into practice two simple techniques he teaches. That's what I love about Alan's approach, he keeps it simple and easy to apply."

Holt Condren
Author of *Surf the Woods*

"I've been in the arena of training and speaking for more than twenty-five years. Without question, Alan Hoffler is one of the best trainers and coaches for leaders when it comes to powerful and effective communication. I couldn't recommend him more highly. Being trained and coached by Alan for more than five years, I have become a speaker who understands the power of connection, the value of content, and the significance of conduit."

Dan Britton
Executive vice president of international ministry
Fellowship of Christian Athletes

"Words are powerful in debate, but they can be muddled. Words can be clear and persuasive, but they can be vapid and distracting. Alan Hoffler's training showed me how to eliminate unnecessary oral and visual distractions from the message that I intended to send. Although his training was for oral presentations, I have used it to clean up my written papers as well. Every word or phrase that does not directly convey a message or an emotion is a distraction from the power of my speech or debate. While I am an imperfect student of Alan's training, I profited immensely from it."

Paul Stam
Attorney

"The one word describing my feelings after [Alan's] training was 'hope!' I identified my growth areas and practice strategies. This training and the information in this book alone won't make you better. It will make you aware. It will give you tools. If you will decide to purposefully practice you will improve (greatly). You will grow (a lot). You may even join the list of great presenters!"

Mark Hull
Certified presenter, 3Dimensional Coaching

DEDICATION

This book is dedicated to all the students, colleagues, and friends who were willing to get on stage to present, teach, and share. I've learned from you, and I owe much of who I am to those who have gone before.

ACKNOWLEDGEMENTS

Thanks to:

Those who gave me an opportunity:

- Dr. Walt Christy, for hiring an under-qualified, 22-year-old hothead based solely on his trust in me.
- Dr. Robert Martin, for his advice and willingness to take a chance on me.
- Ellen Daniels, for buying my explanation: *"The job description said you want someone who can think analytically. That's me."*
- Bart Queen, for opening my eyes to what I could be as a speaker and teacher.
- Don Sandberg, for making a space and giving me freedom and support when there were others more qualified and in line ahead of me.
- Kevin Murphy, for putting me in front of all those audiences, and then taking the bullet when it didn't go as planned.
- GB, for having the naiveté to believe I was a professional speaker and then sparking the belief that I could be one by hiring me.
- To the many students of MillsWyck Communications workshops. You didn't know you were guinea pigs for many of the exercises. Thanks for being willing participants as we learned together.
- Jeff Bailey: All those lunches, ideas, phone calls, and phrases of *"I've about decided..."* helped to form the ideas

that spawned the vision for this. Oh yeah, and thanks for the domain name, even if I did forget you owned it before I did.

Those who encouraged me to write, especially:

- Tom Rosenak, for buying the first copy, before it was ever written. It's not often that we chance into a kindred spirit, but, brother, I am blessed for that introduction.
- All the authors in Born Toastmasters, who gave advice and inspiration to join the tribe of "published author."
- Karin, your magic with an outline is amazing. Thanks for making my 80,000 words into 52,168 that said what they needed to say.
- The many eyes who helped edit the manuscript.

Those who supported me unconditionally:

- Mom and Dad, who continue to pray, offer their ears, and spend hours proofreading. You done good.
- Allyson and Joel—little Mills and little Wyck—I can always count on a big hug and time for one more game of Five Crowns. You are a blessing to me. I'll do everything I can to give you the platform to make your mark on the world. I love you more than you'll ever realize.
- Haley, for changing course, over and over, for better or for worse, and never doubting (at least out loud) that we could make it, together. I love you.
- And most of all, to the Author and Perfecter of my faith, for being the ultimate example of Rule #1.

Alan, Fall 2015

TABLE OF CONTENTS

INTRODUCTION

How This Book Came to Be

I graduated from college with an engineering degree, then promptly set off to change the world—as a high school math teacher.

I was horrible at it. Boring lectures. No interaction. Shaky discipline. Poor planning. I survived Year One because I was stubborn, worked hard, and didn't know it was an option to quit before the school year was over. There was no Year Two. I blamed the students. After all, they were bad students. Dropouts. Cut-ups. Problem kids.

After a few years as a teaching assistant in graduate school, I again landed a job as a math instructor, this time at the college level. While it was far more enjoyable than teaching high school—the students were now motivated or they flunked out—my teaching skills still left much to be desired. I lectured to the blackboard, went way too fast for students learning calculus, and spoke with a lovely monotone. When the contract expired, I needed to find a way to make a living. Apparently teaching math was not part of the equation.

It was on to Corporate America, where I found myself in the training department of a large software company (or rather, departments—I got reorganized ten times without ever changing jobs). While there, I not only received education on how to teach and present, I got a lot of practice. More importantly, I uncovered an insatiable desire to become good.

My transformation started with a multi-day class that gave me all the tools I needed to be an exceptional communicator and presenter. Though I'd been humbled at how poor my previous skills were (proven through an excruciatingly painful video of my slouching, rocking, mumbling self), I was eager to use the revelatory new techniques I'd been taught.

When I went back to the real world, a stark realization hit me: average speakers in the real world are not...very...good. In fact, the average presentation is just plain poor. Monotone voices. Predictable, trite, and mostly useless content. Bored audiences. Empty discussions. A few platitudes and *"Nice job"* comments, then off to the next meeting, presentation, or speech.

What bothered me most was no one seemed to care. More meetings, follow-up presentations, and after-action reviews. The following week, month, or year, the same style persisted.

It was rare for anyone to stand out, but when someone did, I noticed. I now knew why I liked some teachers better than others. It was obvious why some (few, but some) meetings captured my attention and I actually wanted to attend. The presenter had skills.

I started a note-taking campaign to discover the difference between the good and the not-so-good speakers. I took notes in schools, churches, break rooms, and board rooms. I observed speakers on TV shows, ball fields, and political stumps. I asked one basic, two-part question: What works, and what doesn't?

It wasn't hard to categorize speakers with this system. Some obvious truths showed up rapidly. I began my list of what to do— and what not to do.

Then I had to ask, if I know what speakers *should* do, how could I train myself and others to do it? The answer was again very simple: we become great by removing the bad behaviors, by eliminating the sins in our presentations. It's not complex. It's not even hard to uncover. Apparently, it can be difficult to do.

Those many pages of notes coalesced into a model with clear indicators of what it takes to excel on the stage. I wanted to create "The Ten Commandments of Presenting." (Commandment One: "Thou shalt not be boring.") I was on to something special, perhaps the first to ever articulate the true secrets of greatness, or so I thought.

When I asked others about my observations, no one denied the validity of my complaints, but there was a shrug of the shoulders and a *"That's just the way it is"* air to dismiss my concerns. *"But it doesn't have to be this way!"* I wanted to shout.

I left my corporate job to found MillsWyck Communications, where we push clients to discover their best presentation self. For the past decade, I've continued to incorporate my observations and the expertise of others into a digestible, understandable system for changing a speaker's habits. I've worked with some incredibly motivated and talented people, who have helped me hone my own speaking style and craft (yes, the teacher learns from the students as well as from other teachers). I'm thrilled to say that the speaker you see today is fundamentally different from the one who punished 150 high school students with some of the worst math lectures ever given.

My ongoing observations and note-taking have not changed my initial conclusion: presentations as a whole are still pretty horrible. Sinful, even. I now have a vision for how to change the presentation universe, and I've made it my mission to touch as many people as possible with the oddball notion that anyone— ANYONE!—can engage, entertain, and educate an audience and move them to action.

Even though I speak regularly all over North America, I still don't view myself as a "great" presenter. Self-perceptions die hard.

However, in removing some of the most severe sins from my own presentations, I've proven it can be done.

I am absolutely convinced you can do it too.

What's all this about *Sin*?

Do I have to use the word "sin"? Most people associate sin with a moral or religious mindset. And that's one of the definitions dictionary.com offers (as a noun): "any act regarded as a transgression, especially a willful or deliberate violation of some religious or moral principle."

But this book has nothing to do with pushing morals on you. I even checked with my atheist friends to make sure I wasn't crossing a line with the imagery. I promise we won't discuss religion.

Another definition of sin (verb) is: "to offend against a principle or standard."

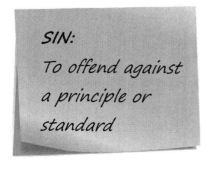

SIN:

To offend against a principle or standard

That's what we're talking about. For sin to take place, a standard must exist.

What then is the standard against which presentations are judged? This question must be answered before we can correct our missteps. Two follow-up questions quickly emerge:

1. What can a presenter do that would be offensive?
2. Must a presenter be willful to offend, or might these behaviors be unconscious actions?

The answers to these questions, supported by thousands of presentation observations, guided my beliefs on communication and created the premise for the solutions this book offers:

- There IS a standard.
- Violating that standard is offensive to anyone listening.
- You don't have to know you are offending to be guilty.

So, yes, sin is an appropriate word for the actions of most presenters. This book is my attempt to help you avoid the easy trap of presentation sins, and gain the respect and attention of your audience, no matter the situation.

What to Expect from This Book

This book is based on the series of workshops taught by MillsWyck Communications. If you've taken one of our workshops, you'll find this book a handy reference guide with reminders of the core elements you learned. If you're reading on your own, and even if you're an experienced presenter, you'll find valuable nuggets to advance your skills.

The Foundation chapter offers an overview of the MillsWyck approach, and the subsequent chapters delve into more detail on the three main aspects of powerful communications: Conduit, Content, and Connection. The Conclusion wraps up with a few final thoughts on bringing the Three Cs together.

Throughout the book watch for:

- **Definitions** – We have to know what we're talking about.

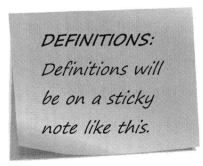

DEFINITIONS:
Definitions will
be on a sticky
note like this.

- **Sins** – In each chapter we include some of the most common presentation sins, and turn them into…

- **Tips** – Insider secrets to make the skills easy, or at least doable.

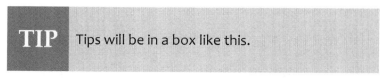

TIP — Tips will be in a box like this.

At the end of the book you'll find additional resources and a detailed table of contents for easy reference to specific topics in the book.

Your mind may wander. Let it. Better yet, take out a pen and write down your ideas. I did, and you're holding the result.

Whether you're a math teacher, preacher, comedian, executive, manager, salesperson, technical guru, or a parent, this book offers simple tools to enhance your communication—and, by extension, your world.

FOUNDATION:
LAYING THE GROUNDWORK

What do we mean by *Presentation?*

In the business world, the word *presentation* has somehow acquired the meaning "collection of content almost always contained in a computerized program." The de facto standard is Microsoft PowerPoint, although Apple's Keynote, the open source Impress, SlideShare, and Prezi, and a host of other tools accomplish the same basic tasks. This definition is more than a little flawed. We need to establish what should—and should not—be considered a presentation.

Would an interview be considered a presentation? A weekly group meeting? A short devotional? A drill on how to conduct a full court press in basketball? Helping a child with trigonometry (ooh, now THAT would be fun!)?

The view we take in this book is much broader.

Presentation is any interaction where one human communicates to another.

Presentation includes all of the examples above. It also includes complaining to your HOA, crafting an email to your child's T-ball coach, leaving a voicemail with a prospect, and testifying before Congress. The guidelines we discuss in this book apply to every communication situation you encounter.

At MillsWyck Communications, we take such a broad view of "presentation" because humans are prone to compartmentalize. We filter out and ignore important principles. The way we *think* about communication is often the root problem. If you believe that a presentation must involve a projector, a particular audience, a standing presenter, and a microphone, then you're going to approach that event differently from everyday communication interactions. You prepare for a formal presentation but not for a dinner conversation. Why not prepare for the dinner table too? The skills you develop in the comfort of your own kitchen apply just as well to the corporate board room. And the attitude you take with your kids can easily seep into your unscripted Q&A with clients.

PRESENTATION: Any interaction where one human communicates to another

Instead, I invite you to view each time you open your mouth as an opportunity to apply the core principles of communication and become better at using them. You are always "on."

Why is presentation excellence important?

When observing presenters, it quickly becomes apparent that excellent skills are not required to be "successful." CEOs, pastors, senators, keynote speakers, actors, TV hosts, and Hall of Fame athletes frequently are poor speakers. This troubles me. If communication skills aren't the secret to their success, why should we mere peons attempt to master the craft?

I personally have two main reasons that have nothing to do with the amount of money I earn or the awards I accrue.

First, I want to be better. The challenge of speaking well has flamed a passion inside me that cannot be quenched. I never want to settle for mediocrity.

Second, I want my message to outlast me. I want the impact I have on the world to be measured beyond my lifetime. I want to make sure that those I touch will use the words I choose and actions I exhibit to achieve greatness in their lives. What a thrill to think that great-grandchildren I'll never meet will declare, *"My great granddad used to say..."* What satisfaction there is in knowing that a business will be changed by leaders who care enough to communicate well.

Communication matters. What are you saying?

Why do we struggle with presentation excellence?

If the fear of public speaking were, as Seinfeld claims, greater than the fear of death, then we'd have managers swan-diving from boardroom windows to avoid their update with the executive team. We'd have conference chairpersons lingering in front of a bus on their way to the convention hall. We'd have actors jumping from the catwalk rather than walking on stage.

Even so, fear is one of the main factors that cause us to struggle with presentations, especially with *formal* presentations. Even people who communicate and present for a living face fear. Or stage fright. Or anxiety. They learn to manage it.

But I don't believe fear is what causes most people to struggle with presentations. I believe most people simply never receive good instruction.

I've had people with master's degrees in speech communication tell me they never learned how to manage a room layout or the importance of eye contact. I've watched CEOs take the stage with no idea how to hold the microphone. I've read books that suggested the way to remove *ums* and *ahs* from your speech was to put a sticky note in your speech outline that said *"Don't say 'um'!"* I've had arguments online about whether hands in pockets should be allowed. I've had students tell me that PowerPoint is great because it keeps them from ever forgetting what to say. I've had nervous people tell me what drug works best to relax them and overconfident people tell me there's no situation in which they'd ever be scared.

Where did they learn this stuff?

Whenever I find someone who is excellent at communicating, I always ask the same question: *"How did you get to be so good at presenting?"* When I started making this inquiry, I wanted to hear, *"Who me? I'm just good. I was born to do this!"* But no one has EVER offered that explanation. Instead, EVERY SINGLE presenter could tell me the time, the place, and the person who was instrumental in developing his or her skills. That leads me to believe this very important point:

Speaking well is a skill that can be LEARNED by anyone.

If speaking well can be learned, there's hope for people like you and me. We can learn this. We can do this. We can stop sinning against our audiences and start impressing them instead.

The Unbreakable Standard: Rule #1

If sin means to offend against a principle or standard, we must clearly identify the standard. In this case, it's an easy definition, but it's difficult to accept, almost impossible to live out, and trivial to violate. I call it "Rule #1" (creative, right?!).

Rule #1: It's not about YOU.

Presenting is not about you, the presenter. Presenting is about the audience. That's the rule. That's the standard.

This standard is not what modern culture teaches us. Business schools, self-help books, motivational speakers, and even our parents often teach us just the opposite. We may SAY we believe in this standard, but our actions frequently prove the opposite.

It's not about YOU. When we are communicating—no matter the message or the environment—it's NOT ABOUT YOU. Whatever you do when you present, train, speak, motivate, inform, or entertain, it should be done with the audience's best interests in mind. When we fail to consider the audience's needs, we are in violation of the standard. It's a sin. You may not even know you're doing it. It's still a sin. It may not feel bad; it might even feel good. Still a sin.

And here's the real kicker... If Rule #1 is true, you don't even get to decide if you've sinned or not. That's for the audience to determine. As we examine the most common presentation sins in this book, they all come back to the violation of this simple standard: the presenter has failed to make the presentation about the audience.

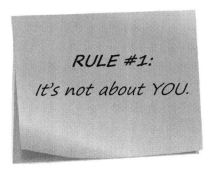

The Corollary: Rule #2

If you're in London Underground, as the train doors are closing you'll hear the announcer (a wonderful, polite lady with a lovely accent) alert you by saying, *"Mind the gap!"* In other words, pay attention to the gap—don't get caught!

It wasn't long into my speech coaching career that I noticed my clients arguing with me. I'd give some feedback or a suggestion and they'd respond, *"That doesn't feel right."* Or I'd comment about how briefly they paused and they'd say, *"That was an eternity."* I remember my own journey and having to come to the realization that the way it *feels to the speaker* is not necessarily what the *listener sees and hears*. The difference between these perceptions is call "the Gap." Our second rule directs us what to do when we recognize the Gap. In presenting, we must pay attention to the gap between what we feel and what our audience experiences. They are not the same!

Perhaps the biggest gap a presenter experiences is time. A pause of two seconds seems like an eternity to a presenter, while the audience feels like it is just enough time to process the last sentence. To a presenter, the time to walk from the side of the stage to the computer feels like one of those dreams where your feet are stuck in the mud and you can't run to escape the approaching zombie horde. The audience, on the other hand, sees your pace as quite normal and relaxed. They enjoy the break.

Soft-spoken presenters, when asked to raise their voices, feel like they're yelling, while the back row of the audience is delighted they don't have to strain to hear. Standing straight when you're used to slouching at your desk might feel awkward, but the audience sees a natural posture. Gesturing above your shoulders may feel like wildly flapping your arms, but the back of the room is happy they can see what you're doing.

Regardless of how it feels, we've got to find out what works for our audience. Always go back to Rule #1: It's not about you. But the corollary also means your stomach can be fluttering while the audience sees a confident, poised speaker.

The Difference between Good and Bad

We begin our workshops by dividing up the class participants into two groups. One group brainstorms characteristics of great speakers; the other group brainstorms characteristics of not-so-good speakers. The lists are amazingly accurate—and completely useless.

In the first hour of the workshop, the students prove they already know almost everything they will learn. More knowledge is not the answer to becoming a good presenter.

We then discover another amazing truism. Every one of the characteristics of a great presenter has a corresponding entry on the not-so-great list. All it takes is a negation to make a skill change lists.

Bad list	Good list
Monotone	Not monotone
No emotion	Expresses emotion
Rambling	Clear structure
Runswordstogether	Pauses
Runs over	Ends on time
Reads slides	Speaks to audience
Uses filler words	Clear speech
Facts only	Interesting stories
Looks all over	Eye contact
Stationary	Purposeful movement
Reads slides	Great visuals

This observation leads us to another question: How can we stop the behaviors that are wrong (the sins), and replicate the behaviors that are correct?

The answer is the most important lesson you will read in this book.

You become great by:

1. Learning what you need to do.
2. Doing it with ongoing instruction and concerted practice.
3. Putting yourself in situations that require the use of the skills you are learning.
4. Relentlessly evaluating (e.g., watching video of yourself) and correcting every nuance of your behavior with respect to what works for the audience.

Athletes will immediately recognize this process. Learn. Practice. Play. Review.

Wash. Rinse. Repeat.

The Tennessee Titans football team used to have emblazoned in foot-high letters around their practice facility:

**A professional is someone who knows what to do...
and DOES it!**

Almost everyone *knows* how to be a great presenter. Very few actually do what they know. That's what makes the difference.

The Three Cs Model

When it comes to presenting well, there are three elements that cannot be ignored: Conduit, Content, and Connection. We'll take a quick look at them now, then explore each of them further in following chapters.

Conduit: Your Communication Channel

A conduit is a channel. Often it's a pipe that carries electrical wire or a fluid. It transmits an important entity from one place to another while protecting its load from outside influences. That's exactly what the Conduit does in presenting as well. The Conduit is our channel for giving the audience information while protecting them from distractions that hamper communication.

The Conduit is made up primarily of the physical elements a presenter uses: posture, eye contact, pauses, facial expressions, gestures, vocal variety, movement, and room logistics. Using these skills correctly allows the audience to give their full attention to the message.

The Conduit is the domain of hands-on training. Just as you wouldn't expect a child to learn to throw a baseball from reading a web page on the subject, or a teenager to learn how to drive without actually getting behind the wheel of a car, you can't develop Conduit skills by reading a book. You have to practice them.

Content: Your Communication Message

"Content is king." Without good content, you will struggle as a presenter. If you have nothing to say, why should the audience listen to you?

Have you ever heard a speaker successfully explain a complicated concept to a lay person? Are there lessons from elementary school you remember decades later? Or have you seen a presenter who was clearly a subject-matter expert, but couldn't parse a clear sentence? Do you recall a time when a speaker rambled so far afield you couldn't remember the original topic?

Content is more than what we say. Content includes organization, length, emphasis, repetition, context, and applicability to the situation and the audience at hand. Content is what your audience will repeat and remember.

Connection: Your Communication Relationship

We've all had teachers who knew their subject and organized their lectures well. We've seen speakers who were skilled. But sometimes, there is a little extra. A *je ne sais quoi*. Charisma. The "it" factor.

The last element of our Three Cs model is Connection.

Connection is where we acknowledge that we are talking to humans, that there has to be some element of relationship in our communication. Connection involves our emotions, our will, and our mind. Connection may be hard to put our finger on, but we know when it's missing.

Connection may come through stories or humor. It may come through powerful images. It may come through a probing question. You can connect by using common language or just saying the one phrase an audience member came to hear.

We want to believe that people who have "it" are born that way, that they possess some inner character trait that gives them an inherent advantage at communicating. But like most traits we admire in others, Connection can be cultivated and improved.

Bringing the Cs Together

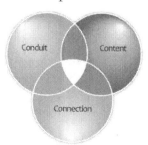

You can have every skill honed. You can pause, smile, gesture, move, and vary your voice with world-class precision. But if you have nothing to share and don't move your audience, you are a huckster, a politician (with apologies to the wonderful public servants I've met, but that's the stereotype). It takes more than a Conduit to make a great presenter.

You can be the smartest person in the room, versed in every point, organized, factual, and clear. But if you're boring, fumbling, and lifeless, you've entered the domain of the engineer or academic (I speak from experience—engineering degree, remember?). It takes more than Content to make a great presenter.

You can be the life of the party, know everyone in the audience by name, make them laugh, and move them to tears, but if you're a mess to watch and have nothing meaningful to say, you're just an entertainer. It takes more than Connection to be a great presenter.

Miss any of the Three Cs and you'll break Rule #1 (It's not about you!). You will sin against your audience.

But when you combine all three elements—Conduit, Content, and Connection—you have entered the sweet spot of presentations. Your audience will want to listen, will think highly of you, and will remember what you say. That makes you a success in the eyes of those who matter most—your audience.

CONDUIT:
YOUR COMMUNICATION CHANNEL

What do your actions say?

Stephen M. R. Covey, in *The Speed of Trust*, says "*We* (the speakers) *judge by intent; they* (the audience) *judge by observable behavior. You need to declare your intent to actively influence the conclusions others draw about your behavior, or they'll make their own assumptions.*" This is a huge gap—the difference between our heart (intent) and our actions (what the audience sees).

This is a key truth for speakers everywhere. Audiences judge you based on what you DO. You can be a mess inside. Know nothing about the subject. Be sick as a dog. Hate the very thought of public speaking. But if you execute on the skills in this chapter, you will be seen as confident, passionate, and professional.

The Importance of the Conduit

We described the Conduit earlier as primarily the physical elements a presenter uses: posture, eye contact, pauses, facial expressions, gestures, vocal variety, movement, and room logistics. Using these skills correctly:

CONDUIT:
A channel that transmits items of importance.

- Eliminates distractions so the audience can give their full attention to the message, and
- Gives the audience the impression you want them to have of you and your topic.

If your behaviors cause your audience to talk about what you did rather than discuss what you said, something is wrong with your behaviors (something may also be wrong with your content, but let's save that for the next chapter). And, regardless of what you say, your behavior will give the audience enough information to evaluate you and make up their minds what they think.

Most speakers have three basic perceptions they want their audience to have. They want to be seen as:

- Confident
- Passionate, and
- Professional.

The specific words may vary, but the motivation usually can be boiled down to one of those three areas, so let's take a look at them in more detail and talk a few "Thou shalt not's."

To Show Confidence, Demonstrate Control

Most people who come to my classes or ask me to coach them want to be more confident in their speaking. I have bad news for you: I cannot make you more confident. Only you can do that. Confidence is the belief in an ability. If you don't *have* the ability, you won't be confident. And if you don't *believe* in your ability, you won't be confident. (Someone who believes he has ability and does not is called *over*confident and is headed for embarrassment.) Ability and belief are *both* required.

I also have good news for you: the audience only wants you to *appear* confident. Thus the sin that we wish to avoid is the *appear-*

ance of lack of confidence. It is quite possible to look confident when your heart is pounding. You can exhibit poise even when your mind has great doubt. You can train yourself to *act* a certain way, regardless of how you *feel*. Remember Rule #2: Mind the Gap!

What does a speaker need to do to appear confident? Three main techniques (and they aren't independent of one another):

1. **Poise** – A sense of physical ease and grace
2. **Pause** – The silence between thoughts or sentences
3. **Eye contact** – Meeting the audience members' eyes with your own

We group these three skills into a category we call *control*. A speaker who is under control will be seen as confident and worthy of an audience's attention. Note that all of these skills are independent of a speaker's true confidence. You may be the most nervous person in the room, but if you execute on these three skills—poise, pause, and eye contact—the audience will be convinced you own the stage.

Poise

A confident speaker holds himself with poise. A major component of poise is posture. The speaker *looks* at ease and in control. There is no rocking, fidgeting, or distracting behavior. The speaker's body exudes control. The body's geometry is square and balanced.

Let's start the discussion with the postures to avoid. Each of these has a connotation to the audience that drives a negative impression.

The **Coach** is comfortable for the speaker, but connotes not only authority but perhaps aggression. It is unbecoming for extremely large persons, and can be intimidating when done in proximity to the listener. Save the Coach for the ballfield.

The Coach

The **Clasp** is the most popular default position. Virtually everyone who has not been trained to stand another way will default to some variation of it. The posture has several shortcomings, most notably that it looks weak. It also promotes fidgeting with the hands and limits the use of effective gestures.

The Clasp

The **Pray-er** is a variation of the Clasp, only the hands tend to move more, because they aren't connected. Again, this is a weak and pious posture that does not convey authority.

The Pray-er

Parade Rest is trained by militaries worldwide. Soldiers and seamen can stand for hours (don't lock your knees!). It's comfortable and sends a message of such. But it also attracts audience attention to the midsection (as opposed to the face), limits gestures, and causes doubt in cultures where the showing of hands is considered polite.

Parade Rest

Arms Crossed sends a strong message of disinterest. You may just be cold (temperature) but the audience sees you as cold (temperament). This is an especially bad posture when accompanied with a statement like, "I'd love to hear from you. What questions do you have for me?"

Arms Crossed

The **Fig Leaf** draws attention to parts of the body that most speakers do not wish to highlight. In addition, it tends to draw the body in on itself, reducing the command presence, height, and impact the speaker projects.

Fig Leaf

Hands in pockets is a great argument among speech coaches. I've heard some say it should never happen; others coach it as a strategy. I side with the latter. Putting your hands in your pockets is casual. It should be reserved for audiences where casual is appropriate. If you use pockets, the hand(s) should be completely in the pocket—no dangling thumbs or flapping hands.

Pockets

Women's clothes are not usually designed for hands in pockets, so that limits the opportunities. Also, jeans pockets are usually angled up, which places the arms at an awkward position. Slacks are better. Finally, if you put hands in pockets, don't leave them there long.

What's left? If arms can't be crossed, aggressive, fidgeting, or hidden, the only place left is at your sides. Let gravity run its course. Let your arms fall. Take a **Neutral** stance.

Additionally, feet are in a balanced, relatively narrow stance—no wider than a few inches or the width of your hand. Between gestures, hands come to rest in a relaxed position at the side. The

Neutral

speaker periodically "resets" his position: for a moment, he stops in a balanced stance, arms to the side, facing the audience, pauses...then proceeds.

We just eliminated all the rocking, fidgeting, and distractions related to posture. You still have to address other elements (which we'll get to next), but your first impression will be one of poise.

It's worth a final note that this posture does not *feel* natural. It feels crazy. Unbalanced. Stiff. But coupled with the other skills, it will yield the result of making you *look* great. Mind the Gap!

SIN: Happy Feet

Before I learned the skills you are reading about, I was a swaying, leaning, moving mess as a speaker. In one video from my pre-enlightenment era, I was standing in front of a screen that gave a very nice vertical visual. In just a little over two minutes, I rocked from one side of this vertical reference to the other 74 times. In two minutes! I should have issued Dramamine to my audience.

TIP Plant your feet firmly on the ground and stay balanced. Move only with a distinct purpose.

SIN: Toe-popping

This habit crops up mostly with women in heels. The weight shifts to one leg, the opposite foot rocks back on the heel, and the toe points to the heavens as the rest of the body struggles to find its balance. In addition to the distraction to the audience, I imagine this position is difficult to keep stable and must be tiring.

TIP Keep your entire foot (both of them!) flat on the ground while speaking.

SIN: Fidgeting

A visitor to our home was an anticipated blessing to my family. Except I don't recall anything he said. His behavior was so erratic I could not focus on his message. He squirmed in his chair. He (while seated) played with his keys in his pockets. He grabbed a magazine off the table beside the couch and rolled it, folded it, and swung it so much we had to throw it away after he left. It would not be an exaggeration to say his motion *never* came to a stop during the entire visit. When he left, *I* was exhausted.

When the conversation or thought ends, come to a full stop, a resting position. Do this with intention.

SIN: Leaning

A college instructor had almost the whole package. Moved about the room. Great stories. Clearly knew his material. But there was one annoyance that the students noticed. Whenever he'd go into "thinking mode," he'd lean. On anything. The desks (getting *very* close to the students). The rolling instructor chair (which sometimes had interesting results). The instructor desk (once nearly knocking the computer to the floor). It was as if when he stopped his formal content, his body just went limp. And a limp presenter does not convey confidence in the message.

Stay balanced. Keep your weight off any furniture.

SIN: Grabbing the Lectern

A past President of the United States was in the middle of his weekly press conference. On this particular day events resulted in many more people than usual watching. The President gave his ten-minute briefing, then asked for questions. I always thought the President would get a little love from the press and the first question would be a softball.

I was wrong.

The first question went something like this: "Mr. President, does this event confirm your opponent's view that you are out of touch with the American people and there is a mandate for change in this country, starting at the top?"

OUCH!

Reading a transcript after the event, I thought the President's verbal response was quite decent, if not excellent. But his physical behavior as he answered was telling. He shifted from an erect posture to a lean. He grabbed the lectern with both hands, leaning on the right arm for support, and gripping so tightly with the left you could almost see the blood drain from it. What do you think the nonverbal message was? Not positive, to say the least.

Even when not under attack, presenters have a tendency to hang on for dear life.

I was cured of lectern mishandling by listening to an audio recording of one of my speeches. I kept hearing a loud CLUNK in the middle of my talk. I finally realized it was my hand and wedding ring smacking the lectern. The sound was easily picked up by the microphone. Now I only touch the lectern on purpose when I have a reason, which means rarely.

 TIP Just as in free space, when you speak at a lectern, use a neutral posture with arms at your side. If you gesture, make sure your arms are above the lectern. And then, reset.

Pause

A confident speaker knows how to pause. This is a horribly difficult skill to master, for the better we know our content and the more comfortable we are on stage, the faster we tend to go. However, the more we learn to separate thoughts and allow our silence to carry impact, the more confident we appear.

SIN: Failure to Stop Talking

IfIputasentencetogetherwithnospacenopunctuationandnoendyoull haveamuchtoughertimereadingitandyoumaynotreaditatall.

We have the same tendency when we speak. We don't stop enough.

Not stopping is a sin because your *audience* should not have to decipher what *you* want to say. When people have to work at what should be easy, they quit. Listeners do not want to spend brainpower decoding what you have to say, no matter how important it is.

What's the key? Punctuation. *Honor* the punctuation. Make good use of the comma, period, dash, ellipsis, colon, semi-colon, question marks, and exclamation points (!).

Great speakers stop. Period.

 TIP Count to two at the end of every sentence until you can train your mind to stop. It will seem like an eternity, but the audience will barely notice.

NOTEWORTHY: English Language Learners

For people who speak English as a second language or are English language learners (often referred to as ESL and ELL), being understood when speaking English goes beyond pronouncing vowels and consonants correctly and using the correct rhythm, stress, and pronunciation rules. Learning to pause is tremendously beneficial.

Taking a very short pause between groups of words (called "thought groups") gives your listener the opportunity to digest, take in, and understand what you have already said without having to worry about what you are going to say next.

My clunky way of putting it is, English-speaking ears need the pause to catch up when listening to non-native English speakers, especially those with heavier or less-familiar accents. Likewise, if native English speakers use pauses effectively, non-native speakers can more easily keep up.

SIN: Using Filler Words

A local on-air TV personality was the headliner for an amateur speaker night I attended. Each presenter spoke for exactly five minutes. They ranged from the bad to the predictable to the awesome. This celebrity, who speaks on air to several hundred thousand people at a time, managed to uncork fifty-one filler words in his five minutes, or one every six seconds! Essentially every sentence had its own *um, ah, er,* or *like,* leaving the audience wondering what was just said and what was coming next—and I don't mean in a good way.

I later had a chance to chat with the director of marketing for the station and mentioned the situation in passing. She proceeded to rattle off a list of on-air personalities that they couldn't send out in public, despite their ratings and popularity. Apparently reading a teleprompter with a smile is not a skill that translates to the dais.

TIP Watch a video of yourself or ask a listener what your habitual filler words are. Once you're aware of them, PAUSE when you feel the temptation to say one. It might feel jerky at first, but eventually your speech will smooth out again—without the fillers.

SIN: Using Connector Words

My son's first grade teacher required oral book reports, with essentially one rule: you couldn't start a sentence with "and" or "then." Have you ever tried eliminating those words from your speech? It's HARD! But the kids learned to avoid the sin of using "connector" words.

Students in my workshops quickly learn "so" is also banned (as are "well" and "now"). If they begin a sentence with "So…," I cut them off and shout, *"No SO for you!"* (a Seinfeld reference for all you fans out there!). The frequency of my interruptions indicates how prevalent "so" has become in our speech. Many former students tell me they are amazed at how much they notice "so" in public now that they have been made aware of it.

To be sure, these connectors are valid English words, unlike many of the filler words. And no one is immune from their temptation. I once tried to match a transcript from the White House Press Corps to a YouTube video and was shocked to see how many "flow words" had been redacted!

I've had people tell me that non-words make you sound more "real," more believable. But I assure you, I've never had a client audience complain that the speaker was too polished and not believable.

It *feels* so natural to connect sentences. But if you connect every sentence, what are you not doing? You are not *pausing*. Your listeners need a break. If first graders can beat this habit, the rest of us can do it too.

 Record your speech; listen for the connecting words at the beginnings of sentences. Employ the help of a grade-schooler for accountability in eliminating them when you speak.

Eye Contact

A confident speaker looks directly into audience members' eyes. Not in the audience's general direction. Not toward them. Not floating around them. Not rapidly past them. Not above their heads. She looks directly into the eyes of ONE audience member, then with purpose (and during a pause) moves to the eyes of another audience member. One. At. A. Time.

Most of our students believe they look at their audience's eyes. And they do. They look *at* them. But the difference is that you need to look *into* the eyes of your audience. Not a glance. Not a rapid movement across the entire group. But one person.

Our keyword here is STOP. It references two ideas. First, every sentence needs to stop. Instead of putting a comma, a connective word, and another sentence, STOP. Put a period in place.

Our second STOP is an acronym that guides eye contact. S.T.O.P. Single Thought, One Person. Written thoughts are separated by punctuation. That is what your eye contact becomes—visual punctuation. In this sentence [change eye contact], you'd look at two people [change eye contact]. As you begin a new thought [change eye contact], you also find a new audience member to look at [change eye contact]. Of the three skills we've covered so far [change], posture [change], pause [change], and eye contact [change], eye contact will take the most practice and yield the largest results.

Whew! It's exhausting to have that much purpose to your eye contact. It's much easier to just "spray" your audience. But there is an amazing difference when you use this skill. This is one of the most dramatic demonstrations we make in our hands-on work-shops. A person who is a rambling mess appears to make a transition in just minutes to a speaker full of confidence, poise, and impact. Note we said *appears*. Inside, they may still be a mess, but this gives our nervous speakers a concrete skill to execute, and the results are fun to watch.

Another benefit to this skill is lurking beneath the surface. By using eye contact for punctuation, you create pauses at the proper places. This pause gives you time to think. This pause gives the audience time to digest. And, most amazingly, this pause will keep your mouth from running on and uttering those dreaded non-words. (Um. Ah. Eh. You Know. Like. And. So. I mean. Actually. Basically. Right? Well. Now.)

This is an amazing skill to have at your disposal, and it can be perfected with just a little practice.

SIN: Avoiding Eye Contact

One week before I proposed to my now-wife, I got to attend her family's Big Holiday Gathering. And by big I mean probably seventy-five people! After the meal, everyone slowly moved into one room. Oblivious—I had to be pointedly invited—I joined the group to see the large assembly. There was only one seat left: at the head of the table seated next to the senior member of the family, Mr. Curtis. I later found out that any potential suitor had to be "interviewed" by the senior member of the tribe, while the audience was left to judge the suitability of this prospective mate. Even though I was slow to realize what was happening, I did eventually "get it" and began to act accordingly.

Mr. Curtis was a blue-collar, old-school, hard-working, firm, fair man. At the time, I had just finished my stint teaching college and started a job at a white-collar, yuppie-filled, knowledge company. Our worlds couldn't have been much further apart.

Mr. Curtis asked me all sorts of leading and pointed questions, trying to get a rise out of me and a laugh for the assembly. It was all in good fun, but there was a measure of seriousness to it all. No one in the room (except me) knew of my intent to make this relationship permanent (although I was told later that most had their suspicions).

At the end of the longest five minutes of my life, Mr. Curtis paused for what seemed like days. He finally said, *"I guess he'll do. Alan, I have no idea what you were saying about half the time—you use a lot of big words. But one thing you did: you looked me straight in the eye. To me that means you're a trustworthy fellow. I like that in a man."*

It's been two kids and almost twenty years of happy marriage since that dinner. While Mr. Curtis is no longer at the family gatherings, his lesson has stuck with me. People trust you when you look into their eyes.

 TIP Look at one person—and one person only—for each complete thought you utter. Break eye contact only when a sentence would have punctuation.

SIN: Talking to the Slides

Walk into the nearest corporate office or conference. You'll find presenters standing up to present, giving a few opening words, and then…facing the slides while they speak.

You'll also find the audience tuned out and texting.

I suppose it's a tough task: the screen is on one side of the speaker, the people are on the other side, and the computer with notes is somewhere in between. But the turn of the speaker's head toward the slides has become almost comically predictable.

This behavior is usually indicative of a bigger issue: the presentation has become about the slides rather than about what the presenter has to say.

TIP If you don't have your content fully memorized, it's OK to refer to the slides or to your notes as a prompt. During that refresher, *do not speak.* Before you begin to speak, return your eyes to an audience member. Pause. And continue.

SIN: Holding/Reading Your Notes

At the product launch for the iPhone at MacWorld 2007, Apple CEO Steve Jobs gave one of the most transformational product launch presentations of all time. On stage with Mr. Jobs that day to make the announcement was Cingular (now AT&T) President Stan Sigman. At what was arguably his company's greatest moment, Mr. Sigman walked on stage and pulled out a stack of 5x7 cards and began to read from the cards in a halting voice. He did not finish a sentence without glancing at his notecards. He stumbled over phrases. His voice was monotone. Five and a half minutes later, the audience was noticeably deflated, and for good reason. Until their hero Steve Jobs bounded back on stage to reinvigorate the audience, the largest public message in both companies' history in front of 6,000 people live was on a downward spiral due to the (poor) use of a presenter's notes.

(You can still access videos of this event at YouTube. Immediately following Mr. Sigman's five minutes, Mr. Jobs' remote clicker fails, which is entertaining on a completely different level.)

Whenever possible, rehearse your presentation so you don't need to hold notes. If you must use notes, pause while you refer to them, then make eye contact and continue.

SIN: Staring at Your Feet

Q: How do you tell an extroverted engineer from an introverted engineer?

A: The extrovert looks at *your* shoes when he talks.

(I can tell that joke. I'm an engineer—and one of the few extroverted ones, although barely.)

We laugh at jokes that have a basis in truth. Generally speaking, staring at one's feet (or the ceiling, or the carpet, or out the window) does not engage an audience.

 Head up. Eyes front. Always look at a person in the audience when you speak.

SIN: Staring at One Person Only

In my high school physics class, the instructor had one rule: students were not allowed to talk except to answer a question. The instructor lectured with his back to the class as he scribbled on the chalk board (yes, chalk board—I'm old), turning around only when he heard something. On any given day you could find students reading, sleeping, and even playing chess—as long as they didn't talk. It wasn't a very good learning environment, but once you got the hang of the no-talking rule, it wasn't hard to comply.

One day in class, I made the mistake of staying fully alert and engaged (my normal state was doodling, dozing, or dreaming). At one point my eyes met the instructor's. From that point on, he lectured to me as though it were a one-on-one conversation. No matter how hard I tried to break free, he looked only at me. I felt singled out, and everyone else felt ignored (situation normal for that classroom).

For the rest of the semester, I kept my eyes averted, fearful of locking gazes with him again.

TIP Make eye contact with EVERYONE in your audience, not just those who seem interested. Big audience? Make eye contact with multiple individuals even if you can't accomplish "everyone."

To Show Passion, Demonstrate Energy

Passion is contagious. If you're pumped up about your subject matter, the audience will be as well. Energy can be transmitted.

But I'll stop short of saying passion is required to be a great speaker. If it were, then we'd all find ourselves *very* limited in the topics we could speak about. (I'd have about five subjects. Fortunately, speaking is one of them!) For instance, pricing structure most definitely is NOT my passion, yet there isn't a week that goes by when I'm not asked to discuss it. What behaviors must I show to let my prospects know that I want to serve them, and that I'm worth every penny of my quoted price?

There are three skills that exhibit a speaker's (perceived) passion:

1. **Facial expression** – The feelings expressed on the face
2. **Gestures** – The movement of the body, especially arms and hands, as a means of expression
3. **Vocal variety** – The varying of pitch (inflection), tone, volume, and speed in speaking

These skills are the domain of ENERGY. They are interpreted as a speaker's passion and draw an audience's attention, emotion, and desire. Not only do these energy skills engage the audience, but when used correctly, they alert the audience to the most important words and concepts.

Analogy: As I write this book, I know I want certain ideas to stand out. I want you to know what is important. All 48,000 words can't be equally important. I emphasize key ideas by making some words, phrases, and sentences different from the rest. Sometimes it's a font change. Sometimes, italics. Perhaps all caps. Punctuation. White space. Underlining. You get the idea.

Likewise, a speaker can emphasize certain words and phrases by slowing down, raising her voice, changing its tone, or cocking an eyebrow. These changes offer the listener clues about what is important. (These clues are especially important when the listener is not hearing his native tongue.) We as listeners gain meaning from more than the words. We as speakers want to create a picture of priority in the listener's mind that conveys our feelings (passion) and appropriate emphases.

Again, these energy skills are entirely separate from how much energy the speaker actually HAS. You might have stayed up all night, have a migraine headache, or be physically adapting to a new time zone, but you can still *display* energy, and thus drive the impression that you are *passionate*. Rule #2: Mind the Gap!

Let's take a look at facial expression, gestures, and vocal variety in more detail.

Facial Expression

Faces express emotion—happiness, sadness, elation, joy, surprise, angst, fear, disappointment, discouragement. In normal one-on-one conversation, we tend not to think about matching the expression on our face to the words coming from our mouths—it usually happens quite naturally. When presenting (in the more formal sense of the word), we also tend to assume our heart-felt emotions pour out of our face and into the hearts of our audience with no effort. It's simple, isn't it? Express. Your. Feelings.

I've found that to be anything but the case.

When I ask clients to watch videos of themselves presenting, one of the most common comments is *"I thought I smiled more."*

While the idea of matching facial expression to verbal content is quite simple, the execution can be more difficult. When coaching, I frequently stop clients mid-sentence and ask, *"Do you like what you're talking about?"* or *"How do you feel about this topic?"* Once we understand the emotion intended for the words, I push them to express those emotions on their face, bigger and crazier and more exaggerated than feels natural, until we get the desired result. Remember, the audience in the back row wants to see your smile (or scowl or tears) just as much as the audience in the front row does.

Of course, this approach only works if we have an audience to provide feedback or a video camera rolling. Speakers need objective evidence that they are *not* going too crazy or exaggerating too much. Without an audience or video, speakers say, *"That doesn't feel right,"* and resort to their old habits. But with objective training and feedback, speakers can transform their audience engagement and entertainment, simply by using facial expressions.

SIN: Not Smiling

One of my eldest child's elementary school teachers looked absolutely petrified on parent-teacher night. I chalked it up to her being young and intimidated by the parents (I was old enough to be her parent). But when I got feedback from my kid, it seems that she just didn't smile much—ever. Which is a shame, because kids especially latch on to the emotion of their leaders and need the reassurance that all is well in their world. Adults need that, too, only we've learned to size up situations better and overlook or cope with those that are not to our liking. In this case, I wonder if the teacher enjoyed teaching children; she lasted only two years.

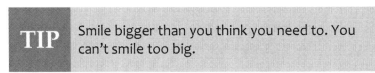

TIP | Smile bigger than you think you need to. You can't smile too big.

SIN: No Animation

I was coaching a contestant in a debate contest. She had gotten feedback that she was stiff and mechanical, and she wanted to know how to fix it. I entered the engagement with confidence—I know how to help someone overcome such characteristics.

Almost as soon as I started giving advice, she blurted, *"That's not how we do it in this competition"* and *"I don't think the judges would look favorably on that."*

I dug a little deeper. *"Tell me about a participant who fared well. What did she do?"* Turns out, the winner did many of the things this contestant was convinced were taboo. When I asked who told her she couldn't be animated and why she felt it was not allowed, it became evident this was a self-imposed belief, not based in fact.

When I was able to show her through video what small facial animations did for her stiffness and lifelessness, this client agreed that her competitive stance would be improved by more clearly expressing emotions.

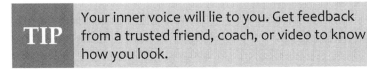

TIP | Your inner voice will lie to you. Get feedback from a trusted friend, coach, or video to know how you look.

SIN: Minimal Expression

I ask students in our workshops, *"Do you think emotion can be transferred from one human to another?"* The answer is always yes.

"Do you think emotion moves people to action?" (Yes!)

"Do you think that expression plays a part in creating that emotion in your audience?" (Yes!)

Then I ask the students to get up in turn and speak on a subject they are passionate about. People choose causes, hobbies, their profession, and places they've visited. The vast majority open with *"The thing I am really passionate about is..."* I ask the students in the audience, *"What level of passion, on a scale of zero to ten, do you see in this speaker?"* Usually the answers are in the three or four range.

I was coaching a group of people who wanted to be professional speakers (people paid solely to give speeches and presentations). One of the students asked the speaker on stage, *"Do you want to be paid ten thousand dollars for your speech?"*

The speaker's face lit up. *"Yes!"* he replied.

"Well, that was worth about a hundred. Give me ten grand this time." I love it when my students coach for me, and in this case, I couldn't have agreed more.

Apparently, speakers who *feel* passion are not usually very good at *showing* passion. This is a problem that is easily overcome with coaching and good feedback from a caring audience.

 TIP Express on your face what you are feeling inside—but BIGGER. Get feedback from people who will tell you what they perceive to be the emotion coming through and how strong it is.

SIN: Forgetting the Gap between Feelings and Expression

When I teach presentation skills in the graduate programs at a local university, we record the students each time they stand up to present. I have the students watch their videos: their initial introductions with no preparation as well as each small session of coaching they receive. The number one comment that they make in their journals is: *"I sure didn't look as nervous as I felt."* It's a living example of Rule #2 and a reminder that what we *show* drives the audience's impression, not how we *feel*.

This works in reverse as well. You may *feel* great, but by fidgeting and moving oddly you can give the impression you are miserable. I watched a pastor tell his congregation one morning, *"I can't think of any place I'd rather be than with you all here today."* However, his non-verbals included crossed arms and backing up while he gave this message. What the assembly likely heard was *"I really don't care to be here today."*

TIP Even when you're nervous inside, you can control what shows on the outside. Practice displaying the emotion that suits your words. Get feedback to make sure they match.

Gestures

Gestures go beyond merely moving your hands and body. Gestures are purposeful and dramatic motions that carry meaning and support the spoken word. Gestures help express individual points and reinforce your overall message.

We enforce two rules on gestures:

1. A (proper) gesture must add meaning to what is said.
2. A (proper) gesture must be BIG.

The first rule is judged with lots of leeway. If it's close, it counts. A sweeping gesture could match the speaker's saying, *"All of you in the audience today..."* or *"As I walked across the field..."* or even *"Look at this mess."* But if you do the same gesture three times in a row, it becomes meaningless movement of your hands and it's distracting.

With respect to the second rule, think this: gesturing is an extreme sport. Go big, or go home. Unless it has meaning that requires otherwise, a gesture should be above your shoulders. Up high where everyone can see it. (To do this, you might have to disconnect your elbows from your side!) If you're not going up high, go broad. Get outside the "strike zone"—that imaginary box in front of us that we tend to limit our gestures to.

Of course, if you are in a one-on-one environment in close quarters, large sweeping gestures would be inappropriate. If you smack the hiring manager in the head while trying to make the point that you have vast skills, you probably won't get the job. But when you're standing in front of an audience, your gestures are unlikely to be too big.

When you're done with a gesture, reset your arms at your side (or on the table if you are seated). This reset makes future gestures seem even bigger, and focuses attention where it needs to be—on your message.

If you wonder how meaningful your gestures are, video record yourself and play it back at an increased speed (2x or 4x). With no sound and rapid movement, you will immediately be tipped off if your arm motions have meaning or not. This can be a humbling exercise, but enormously enlightening for speakers who want to improve.

SIN: Crossing Your Arms

I watched a corporate VP give his quarterly update to staff. When he was done, he said, *"Now it's your turn. Do you have any questions for me?"*

It sounds innocent enough. *Hey, the exec wants to hear from me!* But his posture took a nasty turn as he fired off his invitation for questions. He crossed his arms, took a half step backward, and began to scowl. Predictably, there was silence. Even his berating, *"Surely you people have something more you'd like me to address!"* got no response. Crickets.

His words said he wanted to hear from you. His posture said he was angry and vindictive. What if you misinterpret his non-verbal cues and things turn out badly? Would you take that chance?

The executive missed his opportunity to hear from his people simply because he sent the wrong physical message.

 Use a neutral posture when you solicit feedback. The "reset" posture is neutral—balanced stance, arms at side, head up. And maybe toss in a smile. ☺

SIN: Arm-flapping

In our workshops, one of the hardest habits for students to break is arm-flapping. We have hand signals to remind them to reset their arms. They correct, then after a few more words the arms pop back up and start flapping again. We remind them, over and over, and they laugh and nod their head. *"I've got it this time!"* they say.

It's funny the first few times. Then they get frustrated. *"Do I do this all the time?"* they ask. I refer them to Mr. Canon (a.k.a. the camera). He never lies.

 Video record yourself and play it back at 2x or 4x. If you look like a cop directing traffic, learn to reset those arms at your side.

SIN: Small Gestures

At the other extreme from flapping is the common habit of trying to gesture while keeping your elbows tucked to your side. (Fear of exhibiting sweaty armpits perhaps?)

The audience at the back of the room can't see you unless you get your arms away from your body. This is especially important when speaking behind a lectern.

 Again, record yourself and play it back at 2x or 4x. If you look like a penguin, detach your elbows from your side. Get those gestures up and out!

SIN: Failure to Reset

One of the first faces for new employees in their orientation at a large software company got up and started with an introduction. Casually leaning against the instructor desk, he put his feet wide and rocked from side to side about once every three seconds. He alternated between clasping his hands as if in prayer or fidgeting with his pen, his ring, his notes. His hands were *always moving*. High energy? Yes, but also extremely distracting.

Sadly, that presenter was yours truly for the first thirteen years of my professional career. Those behaviors describe what I did, seven-plus hours a day, in my new-employee training classes. I shudder to think how exhausting it must have been to watch.

Instead, speakers need to "reset" once in a while. Seeing a speaker reset allows the audience a visual pause and a mental pause. Otherwise they don't know the thought has ended (or they don't know that the speaker knows the thought has ended).

 TIP Watch a video of your presentation at faster than normal speed. Your constant movement and fidgeting will become immediately obvious. Remember: Go BIG! And then reset.

Vocal Variety

The third, and perhaps the most fun, skill to exhibit passion is that of vocal variety. You use your voice to give a message, and you can make your voice change in ways that attract positive attention to what you have to say and emphasize important concepts.

Vocal variety entails:

- **Tone** – The pitch, quality, and strength of a voice; the inflection and emphasis used
- **Volume** – The loudness or softness of a voice
- **Speed** – The rate of speech

SIN: Lack of Inflection

Here's a test. Take the following sentences and emphasize the word in italics. Really make it pop.

I didn't cut my sister's hair.

I *didn't* cut my sister's hair.

I didn't *cut* my sister's hair.

I didn't cut *my* sister's hair.

I didn't cut my *sister's* hair.

I didn't cut my sister's *hair*.

How did the meaning change? The *words* are the same. But the emphasis tells six completely different stories. That's the power of inflection.

 Find words in each thought block that need emphasis and change your voice to highlight them.

SIN: Monotone Voice

If I ask a class of workshop participants what less-than-great speakers do that makes them less-than-great, it doesn't take long to get to "monotone voice." Vocal variety also helps to keep the audience's attention and avoid the dreaded "monotone" complaint.

Having watched several thousand speakers, I believe virtually everyone has a naturally monotone voice. Monotone means one tone. Most people speak in their comfortable voice, which is what they think is appropriate. Frequently in our workshops, we uncover a mother, an aunt, or a coach who had a great impact on the client's view of what is appropriate. Sometimes this person hammered home the message "be quiet" or "be bold," which reinforced a particular tone (and also volume, which is related but different).

One tone is difficult for an audience to listen to over time. To get away from monotone, you must become *polytone*, that is, speak with many tones. A loud tone. A soft tone. A chirpy tone. A tough tone. A voice that sounds like your mother when she used to nag you to pick up your room. An uptick for questions. A slower, lower tone when the topic turns serious. It doesn't matter how your tone changes, only that it does.

 TIP Google "behind the scenes voiceover video." How do professional voiceover artists get their voices to change? They ACT. They use large gestures and magnificent facial expressions. Your voice is changed by your face and arms.

SIN: Speaking Too Softly/Too Loudly

A very smart and respected scientist addressed her peers. She began with, *"I have a quiet voice. Please let me know if you can't hear me."* Aargh!

Volume is the most ingrained of all the vocal habits. If you're loud, you're probably going to stay loud. If you're soft-spoken, it's highly unlikely you'll be shouting at the end of one of our workshops.

Usually there's a story behind a speaker's volume. I'm loud. I'm also the third of three children in my family and the most soft-spoken one of the bunch. (Yes, really!) To be heard in my house, you *had* to be loud. And a loud voice is OK, as long as the room is large (and has carpet and drapes to absorb the sound). A loud voice is great for coaching. A loud voice is great for filling an auditorium. But when I want to show concern and make a point that is different from the rest of my speech, I need to get quiet. The difference in volume is what draws an audience in.

If you're soft-spoken (maybe you had a grandmother who chided you for being loud), you'll *never* offend us with your volume. But when it's time for emphasis, you must. speak. up!

In a group workshop I often ask speakers to increase their volume. They respond *"But I'm already shouting!"* and are astonished when the rest of the group looks on in disbelief. They are NOT shouting.

 Learn to manage your volume by getting objective outside feedback, e.g., from a trusted friend or colleague at the back of the room.

SIN: Speaking "Too Fast"

A presentation newbie hit the stage and finished her ten-minute spiel in a record 4:32. When she was done, the exhale made it clear that this was not an event she had looked forward to. (Well, she looked forward to completing it.) It would not be an exaggeration to say that she didn't take a breath the entire time. Apparently she had learned to breathe in through her nose while she talked out of her mouth. If she honored a period, I didn't hear it. If she ever changed her pace, it was to speed up. After about a minute, the audience began looking at one another wondering if this was a joke and if she was going to stop. The stop didn't come until the end, and her speech was nearly impossible to follow.

Roughly half of my students say they've been told they talk too fast. But if you listen to a podcast at 1.5x or even 2x the speed it was recorded in, you can hear every word just fine. I've been told the human brain can listen four times faster than it can speak. If true, this fact means your audience has significant extra brain-power to daydream while you're talking.

 Chances are, you don't talk too fast—you don't stop talking. Pause between sentences or thoughts and no one will complain that you talk too fast.

NOTEWORTHY: One of the Most Misquoted "Facts" You'll Ever Hear about Speaking

Dr. Albert Mehrabian studied messages back in the 1960s. His studies were limited to messages that contained an emotional characteristic when there was a mixed message, for example, someone who says she is happy to be there but sounds bored stiff, frowns, and crosses her arms. Her words say: happy. Her tone says: not so happy. Her non-verbals say: mad. What does the listener believe?

Mehrabian's numbers say that *in a situation where you are giving mixed messages*, the audience will believe the words you say only 7% of the time. The audience will believe the inflection and tone you use 38% of the time, and a whopping 55% of the time the audience will believe what they SEE, i.e., your non-verbal communication. Now as an engineer, I put little faith in the precision of these numbers, but I do believe Mehrabian's conclusions. When the audience sees and hears a conflict of emotion, they are far more likely to believe what they see than what they hear.

Incidentally this brings up a fact I (and many others) struggle with: believability is not based on truth. Believability is based on behavior. People don't act on the truth. They act on what they BELIEVE to be the truth. And what is believable is based on HOW it is delivered more than on the facts themselves. If this were not the case, con men would never succeed. Please use your presentation powers for good, not evil.

To Show Professionalism, Manage Logistics

The last impression we want to leave is that we are professional. We drive the impression of professionalism based on how we handle:

- **Movement** in the environment we're in,
- The **time** we have for our presentation,
- Any **problems or issues** that arise, and
- Our **personal appearance**.

Movement in the Presentation Environment

Since the introduction of computers to presentations, we've added desks/lecterns to the podium to hold the equipment. We've tethered the equipment to a video input, wired a microphone into the whole apparatus, and ended up with what? Speakers who never venture more than an arm's length from their computers.

Of course, in many situations, movement is impossible, impractical, or impermissible. The President should not saunter around the House Chamber while giving the State of the Union Address. The same probably applies to the graduation speaker and the dinner keynote (probably).

But when you can, use ALL of the space that works for your audience. If you're not sure what the space is like and won't have a chance to see it in advance, ask the meeting planner for photos. Map out a successful strategy for presenting to the entire room.

SIN: Staying in Place

In my very first paid public speaking appearance, the setup was about fifteen round tables that seated ten people each, with the lectern at one end of the room. Typically, the room filled up from the rear. The host kicked the program off, saying, *"Wow. This microphone sure is a long way away. You folks look like ants."* Then she gave her welcome. The next person on the agenda was the organizational president. *"Susie was right. You are a long way away."* And another welcome. Three of the four people who spoke before me commented on how much space was in the room.

Next it was my turn to speak. I had one priority on my mind: *I cannot stand at the lectern to speak.* I had to get in the audience's world. And there was only one way to do it. *Move.*

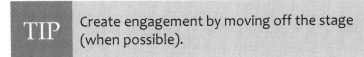

TIP   Create engagement by moving off the stage (when possible).

SIN: Moving without Purpose

I coached a Fortune 500 CEO as he was about to get on stage at his company's signature event. I was prepared—I'd watched the video of the previous year's event. I noticed the guy never stopped moving.

When we started practicing, I asked him why he moved. He didn't even know he was moving. He wanted to look energetic. *Frenetic* was the more appropriate word. He looked like a caged tiger.

We put masking tape on the stage at a few strategic locations. I got him to agree to walk to the X and stop. It completely changed his demeanor. His staff told him he looked calmer and more in control.

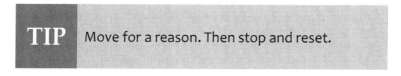

TIP   Move for a reason. Then stop and reset.

SIN: Lopsided Attention

It was my first webinar. The host who invited me to speak had gathered a live audience in the room, and was piping the content to an Internet audience as well. After many years of teaching students in a classroom, I soon resorted to old habits and looked (with one-by-one eye contact) at those who were present. At the end of the presentation, a webinar attendee commented, *"I've seen you speak before and was looking forward to feeling included, but you only looked at the live attendees. I wanted you to look at the camera—to look at me."* Aargh!

I've seen others speak exclusively to the side of the room that had more people in it. I've watched coaches speak only to the starters and ignore the rest of their team.

Ideally, everyone in the room feels spoken to. Done well, each person will feel you focused *too much* on them!

Prior to your presentation, assess the space and set-up so you don't forget to look at the camera, the balcony, and so on. Include *everyone* in your audience.

SIN: Backing Up

In our Q&A workshops, we ask attendees to bring the top three questions they do *not* wish to be asked. It's a fun way to address the most difficult questions we can anticipate, and teach the Q&A methods you'll learn later in this book.

A 20-year veteran of industry got up to practice his answer to a difficult question. As he covered the statement of fact, he began to back up. I immediately stopped him to question the validity of what he was saying. He sheepishly admitted the material was new and he wasn't sure of it. He admitted that I had "caught him."

Even though I knew nothing about the subject of his expertise, I read the speaker's non-verbals to identify "bad" information, potentially even an untruth. While I have never read scientific proof, I firmly believe that when people move backward while speaking, they either are not being completely forthright or are not confident with their material. Backing up is the 'tell' that says, *"I don't really believe what I'm saying."*

Imagine an executive who states, *"I'd love to take your questions"* as she backs up. Now imagine that same executive moving forward and uttering the same phrase. It's a different feel.

Move toward, not away. Step in, not out.

Time Management

We all have the same amount of time to use and share in a day. We want more of it. We won't get it. We never get the same moment twice. Time is the most precious commodity humankind can consume.

If you believe in Rule #1, you'll view your audience's time as a precious gift.

SIN: Not Starting on Time

"We'll wait just a minute more to let people get here." "I was expecting Ferdinand to show up, so we'll hold on until he gets here." "I heard that traffic was bad, so we'll wait to see who else shows up."

Starting late is a BIG sin—a violation against those who made it to your presentation, meeting, workshop, class, or breakout session ON TIME.

I recognize that some cultures don't value starting on time. Those can be country cultures or corporate cultures. One of my clients has a corporate culture in which everything starts five minutes late unless it's first thing in the morning—then it's fifteen minutes late! If I had started my workshop at the posted time, it would have been me and one other student (who was hacking away on his laptop and not even remotely interested in my starting). What to do then?

Give the on-time attendees a bonus story. Get them to postulate their biggest concern about the topic. Give them private coaching or information.

But don't reward those who don't show up on time and punish those who do.

 TIP 1) Start. On. Time. 2) If you must start late for reasons outside your control, have a bonus activity for those in attendance at the published start time.

SIN: Not Scheduling Breaks

In a group strategy meeting, the leader soldiered on. One hour. Ninety minutes. Heading into hour two, people began to exchange glances. Some had already excused themselves, presumably to meet bodily needs. The leader made a snide comment about needing to be fully devoted and how important the time together was. But bladders don't care. And rumps get sore.

Finally, someone mustered the courage to ask if there would be a break. The meeting chair seemed surprised and asked the somewhat rhetorical, but quite condescending, *"Do you need one?"* The response was a nervous, but resounding, *"YES!"* It's hard to believe this leader wasn't aware of that need, but as the old adage goes, *"Time flies when you're having fun."* In this case, only the chair was having fun, and the rest were suffering in many ways.

 TIP The presenter should always be aware of time (make sure a clock is visible) and the audience's needs.

SIN: Running Behind Schedule

It was all touching. Every story. But when the first eulogizer started, *"There's no way I can keep this to three minutes,"* I had a feeling it was going to be a long service. Each subsequent speaker, now feeling let off the hook to keep to the allotted time, went longer and longer. Because I had some inside information, I knew that the entire program was to have lasted an hour or so. At a little more than two hours, members of the congregation began quietly slipping out for bio breaks. A prior commitment mandated my departure before the ceremony ended.

One of the biggest frustrations audience members face—in meetings, conferences, workshops, anywhere—is a presenter who does not stick to the timeframe stated. While most people are comfortable with a little give and take on a long agenda, the overall timeframe should be closely managed.

If you're the speaker whose portion of the meeting was delayed by others, it seems terribly unfair. After all, *you* weren't the one who ran over, and you did have fifteen minutes on the agenda. But that won't make your audience feel sorry for you, and it certainly won't stop their tummies from grumbling for lunch.

What to do?

Do what one of our instructors did when he was on the docket as the last speaker before lunch and took the stage with a steaming buffet already visible in the back of the room. He said, *"I've got some great info for you, and I could talk for a while on this. But let me boil it down to two items: all the material is on the web* (he showed the link and pointed it out in the handouts), *and if you'll spend fifteen minutes a day working the process, you'll be an expert in two weeks."* He completed his fifteen minutes of fame in forty-seven seconds and was given local hero status for getting the program back on track. (You'll learn how he knew to do this in our Content section.)

TIP Always be prepared to adjust your timing. Find a way to end your portion of the program on schedule.

SIN: Running Over Time

At a business seminar, the leader made a big deal of honoring our time. She convinced us that there was plenty of time for us to discuss the topic, use our own examples, and still leave on time. We were promised videos of all the lessons in case something was missed. The commitment to leave on time was reiterated more than once.

And then, lo and behold, we get to quittin' time, and she's not done. She asks for five extra minutes. *Asks*. Since it's her building, her seminar, her show, how could any of us have said *"No!"*? She got her five minutes, plus another three, but her credibility and audience interest were lost.

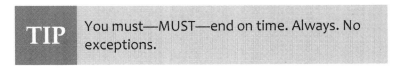

TIP   You must—MUST—end on time. Always. No exceptions.

SIN: Talking About Time

"In the few minutes I've got left..." "This will only take a minute..." "To make a long story short..." (Too late!) *"I don't know how long this will take, but here goes..."*

It seems everyone wants to talk about time, which puts attention on the greatest fear an audience has: the presentation is not worth their time.

Honor the most important commodity we share by *not* talking about it.

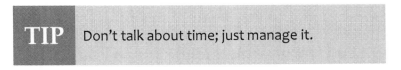

TIP   Don't talk about time; just manage it.

Unexpected Issues

Regardless of their field of choice, professionals perform well even in the worst of conditions. Professionals don't make excuses. They take every opportunity to get better.

A professional handles whatever happens with dignity and ease. Power goes out? Video doesn't work? Cell phone goes off? No problem for a professional. They've been here before (or at least they *appear* to have been here before!).

You have three options when you face an issue:

1. **Fix** it,
2. **Feature** it, or
3. **Forget** it.

OPTION 1: Fix It

Sometimes issues arise that have easy solutions. You drop the pen? Pick it up. Your throat gets a scratch? Take a sip of water. You advance the slides two clicks instead of one? Click back one slide. If the issue you encounter is something that can be fixed so it is no longer an issue, then this is the preferred course of action. Some fixes may take a bit longer, like the battery going dead in your microphone or a need for a drink when you don't have one (why not!?). But they can still be fixed. And should be.

OPTION 2: Feature It

Option two is, unfortunately, the most common approach for many speakers. They draw attention to the problem. We call this "featuring." There are legitimate times when featuring the problem is the correct course of action. For instance, when a jack hammer begins pounding the wall of the room you are teaching in, or the power goes out, or you walk into the room on crutches. Those probably deserve a mention (all have happened to me).

But the more common use of featuring is on issues that should never be brought to the audience's attention. *"I'm not the normal presenter. He called in sick at 5 a.m. today, and I'm not prepared." "I've been fighting a cold and still don't feel very well." "As you can see, my haircut yesterday wasn't a success."* Those may be issues that are at the top of *your* mind, but they have nothing to do with your message or your audience's ability to listen. They are better off left alone.

OPTION 3: Forget It

When options one and two don't work for the audience, you're left with one: forget about it. That stain on your shirt? You're the only one who cares. Just realized you've got the old version of your slides? If the info isn't wrong, roll with it. This is another case of "mind the gap." *You* might know something has gone off kilter, but unless you call it to the audience's attention, *they* (most likely) will not.

SIN: Sticking to the Script When the Situation Has Changed

I tuned in for a friend's webcast. Although I wasn't told how many people were subscribed that day, it was a nationally recognized event with a lot of publicity and potential book sales on the line. While I was particularly impressed with the vocal variety— rate changes, intonations, and volume changes—this presenter was able to employ, it was still obvious that there was a written script, and he was reading every word.

There were two places that the script hurt him. First, there was a technical glitch and a video didn't play. But the script said, *"As we just saw in the video...,"* even though we hadn't. Then there were several homographs that tripped him up. For instance, he saw the word "read" and pronounced it "red," but in the sentence structure it should have been pronounced "reed." This happened several times, which told me and anyone else listening that he was reading without adjusting.

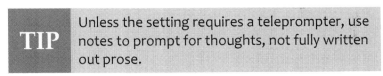

TIP Unless the setting requires a teleprompter, use notes to prompt for thoughts, not fully written out prose.

SIN: Not Having a Backup Plan

There are two types of presenters in the world: those who have had technology fail on them, and those who *will* have technology fail on them.

A software solution sales team showed up to pitch their best-of-breed software. They sauntered in with their shiny suits and polished wingtips and plugged in their computer while the leader of the pack engaged the audience with an intro and corny jokes.

The audience didn't hear anything he was saying—they were too busy watching the comedy show as the suits tried to get the computer to work. (Let's just say this isn't the kind of comedy we'll be shooting for when we talk about humor.)

Twenty minutes, multiple jokes, deflected blame, and numerous apologies later, the computer still wasn't projecting its 16.7 million color image on the screen. The tech lead running the demo offered the suggestion that they use the laptop and those that could see would have the full presentation. When, in the midst of the abbreviated spiel it was noted that most of the audience could NOT see the screen clearly, more excuses and caveats and apologies were forthcoming. Finally, the leader suggested they come back another time. Cue more apologies and promises that *"It really is a great product"* and *"You will be amazed!"*

The audience was already amazed.

 TIP Never rely solely on technology. Always have a plan B that doesn't include technology (white board or handouts, anyone?).

SIN: Not Checking Facilities and Equipment Ahead of Time

A salesperson came in to my former company to do a sales presentation. He walked into the room two minutes before start time. He looked around and asked, *"Where's the projector?"* There wasn't one in this room. A mad scramble ensued, trying to find an alternate conference room with a projector. Since it was apparently a busy day in the company, no room was found; eventually we found a portable projector. His sales presentation was displayed on a whiteboard, about half the size it needed to be, with a crazy glare.

At a breakout session at a national conference, the soft-spoken presenter was interrupted thirty seconds in to her presentation with a loud voice from the back of the room, *"We can't hear you!"*

The speaker momentarily raised her voice, but never directly acknowledged the complaint. Moments later, the same request came again: *"WE CAN'T HEAR YOU!"* The speaker smiled nervously, and again raised her volume for a few sentences, only to revert back to her natural voice within the minute. After another minute of very public discontent and chatting with her seatmate, the person who had shouted out finally got up and left. The presentation went on with almost no audience involvement, even when prompted for questions. Over half the audience was fixated on their cell phones by the end of the presentation, and several more were asleep.

 TIP Research the equipment and facilities ahead of time. Talk to your host or coordinator about what is available. If you must use technology (projector, microphone, etc.), have a backup plan. Better yet, don't depend on technology.

SIN: Not Getting a Drink

In the middle of an impassioned talk, an otherwise very competent presenter got choked up. Not with emotions. *Literally* choked up. Dry mouth. Peanut particle. Hairball. Dust mites.

Suddenly an otherwise engaging speaker was hacking, gasping, pausing awkwardly, and looking very uncomfortable. There was no water at the lectern, but he soldiered on.

For the next fifteen minutes, his voice wandered in and out. He took pauses. Since there was no immediate health risk and the audience was a diverse group of strangers with no one in charge, everyone sat tight. So there was still no water.

The speaker never brought attention to his plight—unless you count his inability to breathe!

 TIP If you are hindered in your message, within reason you should stop and fix the problem.

Personal Appearance

Popular wisdom says that it takes less than seven seconds to make a first impression. It may take even less. Judgments are made in the blink of an eye. One of the first ways an audience determines its impression of someone is by judging how that person dresses and looks. I am not an image consultant, and for most of my life, I cared very little about how I looked. But as a speech coach, I recognize the importance of driving a positive impression based on looks. This includes your hair, your clothes, and your general demeanor. These can all influence your audience before you even take the stage. Unless you are a model, the audience should not be talking about your appearance after your time in the lights.

SIN: Dressing to Distraction

I was one of about 1500 members of an audience, ready for lunch. The speaker was an up-and-comer with a fantastic story.

She had overcome terrible adversity. She started a foundation to help others. Her cause was noble. Her energy was off the charts. She kept our attention the entire time (even with growling stomachs).

But I can't tell you her name. I can't remember her cause. And I don't know what she said that day.

I *do* remember she had multiple metal bracelets on. I think they're called bangles. And she wore a shawl/scarf/sarong thing (I'm sartorially challenged—I don't know what it was) that was wrapped multiple times about her torso and over her shoulder. It kept loosening and falling off her shoulder. Not in a provocative way—she had on an undershirt (I'm sure there's a better name for it). But every time her shawl fell, she grabbed it with her bangled hand and threw it back over her shoulder, banging her bangles (maybe that's why they're called bangles) on her wrist near the microphone and making an awful racket. I doubt I'm exaggerating when I estimate this happened fifty times in her twenty minutes of fame. That's all I can recall.

When the audience remembers you for a distraction rather than a message, you might have met a marketing goal—to be remembered. But you failed on the fundamental communications goal— to be quoted.

> **TIP** Wear clothes that work for speaking. If you're not sure, ask a friend for feedback (ahead of time!).

SIN: Giving the Fashion Police a Crime to Prosecute

Anyone who knows me well knows that I do not masquerade as the fashion police. That's one of the benefits of marrying well and getting older and wiser—you trust people around to make the clothing decisions in your life.

I think the first time a non-family member called me out on my choice of attire was when I was working for the athletic department in college (those who can't play work around those who can). The student interns frequently wore garish clothes, largely because we could. At one nationally televised game, the department's vice deputy calmly informed me that my tie didn't match my shirt in pattern or in color. He didn't condemn; he just said, "*I wouldn't wear that.*" Since I truly did not care about my appearance at the time, it would have been easy to write him off, but the comment stuck with me. It was the first of many incremental discoveries about the appropriateness of what I wear.

But it doesn't take an image consultant to know when someone has overdone their clothing choice. Whether clothes don't fit, patterns don't match, colors clash, or styles expired decades ago, if the audience is talking about your clothing when you finish presenting, you probably missed your objectives for the talk (unless you are a fashion consultant).

TIP Dress well. If you don't know what that means in practical terms, get help. Even one session with an image consultant can clear up your confusion.

SIN: Dressing Down Too Far

At a high-tech company where I used to work, the dress code was, well...casual. I frequently witnessed people walking down the hall barefoot. During the summer, shorts and T-shirts ruled the day. Winter required a bit more formal attire—jeans and perhaps a sweatshirt, but just about anything and everything was acceptable. In fact, I do not recall one instance where a dress code was ever mentioned or enforced.

As someone who loved to dress down, this environment held great appeal for me. As I started my training career there, I was convinced that I needed to fit in and be like everyone else. Until, that is, an external person I trusted made the comment that speakers should dress slightly above their audience. I decided to try it. I'd wear khakis and a polo on days I taught. Gradually I changed my wardrobe to button downs and slacks, and replaced tennis shoes and sandals with boat shoes and loafers. I found two remarkable side effects. One, I began to take my job and classes more seriously. Two, others began to do the same.

One coworker noticed and began to comment, *"Oh, Mr. Fancy Pants today. You must have class."* I hoped that the statement had dual meaning. People noticed. I began to develop a reputation as someone who worked hard at being a good trainer and took teaching seriously. Because most other presenters did not make this distinction, I got opportunities to speak, teach, and go places that many of my peers did not. I can't say that dressing up a notch was the only factor, but it was certainly a factor for me.

Your dress sends a message. Make sure your audience sees the importance you place on your presentation.

SIN: Bad Hair

A guest lecturer was filling in for my freshman chemistry instructor. He had a sort of mad-scientist look, which worked for the role he held. But the comb-over... Wow.

I don't think anyone would have minded a bad hair day (decade?). But this was not just any comb-over. It dominated his look. Worse, the long strands of hair would fall in his face and he would twist his head in an effort to *sling* them back into place.

It did not take long for the ruthless college crowd to make fun of our kindly professor. He may have been a good teacher—I don't recall.

 Ask someone who is more fashionable than you if your look is OK. Get help and change if it isn't. Men, trust that someone special in your life.

SIN: Overwhelming Fragrance

A man I worked with loved his aftershave. At meetings, we could smell him prior to his arrival. Many complained. He thought they were joking that it gave them a headache. Whether it caused lasting pain or not, it was a palpable assault on the senses.

In a common theme for this section, if the audience is talking about something other than your content when you finish presenting, you have probably directed focus to an inappropriate area.

 Leave the aromatic scents at home. Deodorant is fine. Stop there.

Summary: The Conduit Drives Impression

The Conduit is your communication channel. It entails primarily the physical skills a presenter uses: posture, eye contact, pauses, facial expressions, gestures, vocal variety, and movement, as well as logistics and appearance. Using the Conduit skills correctly eliminates distractions and gives the audience the impression you want them to have: it gives your audience the impression you are confident, passionate, and professional.

To show Confidence, demonstrate Control.

- **Poise** is the physical control you show: using good posture and avoiding fidgeting.
- **Pause** is the verbal control you show: honoring the punctuation in your speech, allowing the audience to absorb what you say.
- **Eye contact** is the one-to-one control you show: meeting the eyes of individual audience members so they feel you are speaking directly to them.

To show Passion, demonstrate Energy.

- Use **facial expressions** that match the words you say.
- Use large visible **gestures** to make your point, then reset your arms to a neutral position.
- Use **vocal variety** to emphasize the highs and lows and the most important points of your presentation.

To show Professionalism, manage Logistics.

- **Move** around the space available to you; don't stay tethered to one spot.
- **Manage time** responsibly; treat it as a gift your audience is giving you.
- If an **unexpected issue** crops up, fix it, feature it, or forget it.
- Manage your **personal appearance** so it offers a positive image rather than a distraction.

In the Conduit the goal is not to *become*, but to *display*. The audience can't tell if you're nervous as long as you exhibit good posture, use eye contact, and pause well. The audience can't tell that you dislike the subject if you vary your voice, smile when you speak, and use appropriate gestures. The audience does not know how you feel inside; they know only how you appear on the outside. In the Conduit we must remember Rule #2: Mind the Gap. This is the secret if you are scared to speak. Change your focus from your feelings—we can't change those quickly anyway—to focus on your behaviors instead. Strive for *competence* above *confidence*.

CONTENT:
YOUR COMMUNICATION MESSAGE

Content is King

There is an adage that says, *"People won't remember what you say, but they'll remember how you made them feel."* That may be true. The temptation might be to chuck Content and focus on emotions and drive our impressions through the Conduit and Connection. I believe that would be a mistake.

The Value of Content

The audience needs content. The budget allowances for next quarter. The steps for populating the metadata server with user IDs and passwords. The five questions to ask in a sales call. The life applications to a passage from a holy book. The request for a change in legislation. The play you want the offense to run. The secret to changing those pesky bad habits (like Presentation Sins!).

Leave out content and only tell jokes, and people will walk out disappointed (unless you are a comedian). Fail to give basic facts,

> **CONTENT:**
> The material communicated to the audience.

and there is no credibility. Miss your promise to the audience and you will not get invited back.

At the core, communication is about the exchange of ideas. You are interested in having your audience walk away with a life-changing nugget from your talk. Nick Morgan emphasizes that point in his excellent book, *Give Your Speech, Change Your World*. If you don't want to change your world—even if the change is simply the way your sales team makes cold calls tomorrow—why bother speaking?

Content is a combination of preparation, structure, knowledge of your audience, interesting and creative methods, insights, information, and timeliness.

The Forgetting Curve

How many lectures of your college English class do you remember? You're probably doing well if you remember a few points. How many figures from that last budget meeting do you recall? Most likely only the ones that mattered to your department. How much of the message do you recall from your house of worship three weeks ago? Step to the head of the class if you remember who spoke; bonus points if you can identify the topic.

In the mid-1880s, the German psychologist Hermann Ebbing-haus conducted studies (on himself) on the human brain's ability to remember. While his methods would not pass the test of scientific rigor required today, I believe his conclusions to be valid. First, he found that the human brain is extremely capable of learning. We are able to take in information at an astonishing rate.

Ebbinghaus then discovered that we are equally capable of forgetting. He graphed his data in a representation that has been labeled "The Forgetting Curve." We begin forgetting almost immediately after we learn something. Ebbinghaus postulated that we forget half of our learning within twenty minutes. This implies you likely don't remember half of what you read in the last chapter (which is mildly depressing for an author to consider). You don't retain information unless you make a concerted effort to keep it, such as taking notes, using flashcards, repeating the information many times, or teaching it to others.

As a presenter, you could be tempted to give *more* information, knowing the majority will be forgotten. But a better solution is to find a way to *control what is remembered*.

What makes good content?

The purpose of content is its transfer to the audience. Presented poorly, it can transmit the wrong message. Getting through the speech isn't success as a presenter. *The audience's repeating what is said* is the measure of a presenter's success.

Successful content must follow three principles. It is:

1. **Simple**
2. **Memorable**, and
3. **Repeatable.**

Simple. Good content is given in terms the audience can comprehend. This varies, of course, by audience. You speak to medical doctors in a different language than you do kindergartners.

Memorable. There has to be some hook or reason for the audience to put their brains to work in order to remember what you're saying. There are many techniques to make your content memorable, the most notable being a story.

Repeatable. The audience must be able to repeat what you are saying. The old youth camp game "Telephone" is a great counter-example of repeatability. Line up ten people. Whisper to the first one a sentence with many details. Have that person whisper the sentence in the ear of the next person. Continue on down the line until the last person speaks the sentence out loud to the group.

The final version of the sentence is usually completely different from the first! This is NOT what you want for your message!

An Overview of the Content Development Process

The calls for help with content continue. The vast majority of coaching requests I receive are from people wanting help *"crafting their presentation."* OK, I can provide that help. I've never found a speech I couldn't improve, even my own.

Many presenters seem to think content is about *"Tell them what you're going to tell them, tell them, and tell them what you told them."* While I ascribe to that as a method of reinforcement, it is not very effective without a few other notable techniques added to the formula.

At MillsWyck Communication, we lead people through a three-step process to create content. It is simple enough, like everything else we have learned, but it may not feel easy. And it is *quite* different from what we see clients doing before we meet them.

To develop effective presentation content, we need to:
1. Find **Empathy**,
2. Find the **Essential**, and
3. Make it **Entertaining**.

In that order. This becomes the core of our presentation.

We then add an **Open** and a **Close** to the core content we just created. By "bookending" our presentation effectively, the message is more likely to be received.

The Content process we use works for more than presentations. It works for meetings, training classes, dates, and sermons. And books. This is the technique I'm using now to organize and create this book.

Core Content Creation

Find Empathy

Great content starts in a place that few people dare to go. It's an introspective journey of discovery. It takes time and hard work. It requires actively putting aside your own self-interests and focusing on...your audience.

Ah, the dreaded Rule #1 that seemed so innocent when we introduced it in the opening chapter comes to bite us now. Failure to know your audience is probably the greatest communication sin of all.

We get to know our audience through Empathy, which is defined as the vicarious experiencing of the feelings, thoughts, or attitudes of another.

Many times, we find empathy through a simple pronoun change. Instead of *"What do I need to say?"* we ask, *"What do they need to hear?"* This process is straightforward and logical—our engineer clients love it because it is so concrete—and it produces an end result that your audience can follow, enjoy, and repeat. It does take time and a willingness to step outside your own world into the domain of your audience. (Incidentally, we are turning this process into a video-based curriculum. Sign up for our newsletter at www.millswyck.com to get updates on our product offerings.)

In order to experience empathy, we need to answer questions. Lots of questions. Initially, this process can feel tedious. When I take clients through this method, they often want to quit. It doesn't feel like they are making progress by just thinking.

EMPATHY: Experiencing the feelings, thoughts, or attitudes of another

They want slides. Notes. Graphs. Charts. But what we all need first is to think about:

1. **Why** we are speaking,
2. **Who** we are speaking to,
3. Their **Objective** (based on the Why and Who), and *then*
4. **What** we will say (finally!).

Understand the Why

The first question to answer is *Why*?

Why are you speaking? Are you the boss? Were you selected? Did you draw the short straw?

Why is your audience attending? Were they forced to attend? Chose to attend? Paid to attend? Couldn't wait to show up?

The more complete the answers you uncover, the better you will be prepared to provide content that the audience will love and remember and repeat. Failure to address this critical question—Why?—will almost always result in dull content and a disconnect with your audience.

Here are some—not all—of the questions we ask when taking a client through this process. It usually takes more than an hour for us to hash this out, and clients are tired and wondering if I have any idea what I'm doing. I promise them I do, and that the product will take shape as we get closer to the end.

- What is your attitude about giving the presentation? Why do you feel this way?
- What's the best outcome from giving this presentation? The worst?
- Why are you the one speaking? Why were you chosen to present instead of someone else?
- Why is this topic important? What are the consequences if the audience doesn't "get it"?

- How did you acquire the knowledge you have on the topic? Why doesn't your audience have it (or do they?)? Is there value in the process of learning it?
- What difficulties can your presentation address/solve?
- What do you have to say that is unique or interesting to your audience?
- What is it like to be in your audience (listening to you speak)? What do you think you need to change about the way you currently present to better meet the needs of your audience?

Done well, the insights from this line of questioning will reveal motivations, attitudes, and factors that reveal your audience's reasons for listening to you. These are critical pieces of the puzzle to put together, and failure to examine the Why of your presentation will lead to Presentation Sin.

Assess the Who

Once we've established the Why, we focus on the Who. Who is in your audience?

Identify the Subgroups

One of the most critical realizations and truths that a great speaker must address is that the audience is not uniform. It is made up of subgroups, and individual audience members usually don't identify for you which group they belong to.

Your audience might be separated by *job title*: managers, technical experts, and sales persons.

They might be different by *attitude*: love the topic, hate the topic, willing to be swayed either way.

They might differ in *knowledge*: experts, familiar, or clueless.

They could differ in *demographics*: baby boomers, young marrieds, or teens.

You need to identify the groups in order to meet their needs.

For instance, when I think about the public speaking workshops I teach in the corporate environment, I can usually count on these three groups being present:

1. Experienced presenters, who are quite capable
2. Novice presenters, who are not usually adept
3. Naive presenters, who think they are much better (or worse) than they are

Knowing how to divide my audience allows me to design training that will meet each group's needs.

Identify the Characteristics of Each Subgroup

Once we have our subgroups identified, we need to know important characteristics of each one. These questions must be asked *per audience group*. The answers may be the same, but please make an attempt to find that out through inquiry, not assumption.

- What is the audience's knowledge of the material prior to your presentation? Rank each group high, medium, or low.
- What major challenge(s) or problem(s) do they face related to your topic?
- What is the typical action your audience will try to solve the problem(s)? What can they learn from failure?
- What is their reason for being in the room?
- What is their attitude about your presentation? About you?
- What questions are they likely to have on your topic?
- What topics or themes resonate with this audience?

Again, these questions are not comprehensive, but we want to know as much as we can about who is in our audience. For a meeting, this process would give us individuals' names, not just descriptions. For a conference breakout presentation, we're making broad assumptions about the people and their motivations. It's worth the presenter's time either way.

Handling Different Audience Subgroups

Our daughter has a September birthday, so we decided to hold her back for an extra year of preschool. This additional life experience gave her a huge edge when she arrived in kindergarten. She was already reading on the first day of school. There were other kids in her class—younger kids—who didn't know their alphabet. When Ms. Sudlow began to teach, what would have happened if she'd taught the same Language Arts lesson to the entire class? At least one parent, likely more, would have been hopping mad. If she'd started teaching the alphabet to the entire class, I'd have scheduled a conference faster than a kid headed to recess. *"What are you teaching my child? She already KNOWS the alphabet!"* And if she'd started class by asking kids to read right off the bat, I expect the parents of younger children would have been equally upset.

All children are NOT created the same. And your audience isn't, either.

When you have a diverse audience you have three options:

1. Separate the groups
2. Teach to one subgroup, or
3. Let one group help you present to the rest.

Separate the groups. This is the best option though not always possible. In kindergarten these are called reading groups. They're labeled something bland like Lions, Tigers, and Bears so there is no stigma about reading ability. The purpose is to separate the students by learning level so the teacher can teach an appropriate lesson.

Teach to one subgroup. If you can't separate the groups, you may have to teach to one. This is true when you only get one shot at the decision-maker. You know there are technical people in the room who want details, but the budget keeper is there only this once and you need her approval to move this deal forward. Talk directly to her. A teacher may have to lecture his class on proper field trip behavior when only one child is misbehaving. The rest have to hear the lecture again.

Let one group help you present. This is the hardest method of all and should only be used if you are skilled at facilitation. In education, it's called cooperative learning. (In the business world, it's called letting the know-it-alls have their say.) As a presenter, you let the knowledge in the room come out from the audience. As a trainer, you extract what is already known instead of lecturing. In the sales world, this is known as a referral or testimony—letting others speak and say what you wanted to say. It's extremely effective and engaging, but many presenters find it challenging without first having guidance and practice.

Regardless of how different your audience subgroups turn out to be, there is great value in uncovering them and analyzing them separately.

Uncover the Objectives

We know the Why—why we are speaking and why the audience is listening.

We know the Who—the subgroups of our audience and their basic characteristics.

Now we combine the two questions to uncover the Objectives for our talk.

1. What do we want to happen *during* the talk? Listen? Think? Change their minds? Feel a powerful emotion? This will become our reason to listen—the rationale we give the audience for listening to us (coming up in the Open Block).

2. What do we want to happen *after* the talk as a result of our presentation? This will become our call to action—the change in our world we wish to create because of our presentation (coming up in the Close Block).

The objectives must again be addressed according to each audience group. You may want the decision maker to sign the check, the technical manager to commit people to the project, and the marketing lead to begin a study on competitors. You may want the cynic to consider a new point of view while asking the champion to spread the word to others. You may want the all-star to share her knowledge with the team while getting the company grump to hold his tongue until the project gains approval. Regardless, each group should have a task you want them to complete as a result of your presentation, meeting, pep talk, or keynote.

The best objectives are measureable. How can we know if we accomplished our goal unless we can say with assurance that we did or we didn't? See the table below for examples of objectives.

Objectives	
Not Measureable	**Measureable**
Discuss...	Give examples
Review...	Make a decision
Give an overview...	Buy the product
Talk about...	Sign up for newsletter
Introduce...	Accept meeting request
Present about...	Accomplish...
Take questions...	Schedule a demo
Wrap up...	Visit our website
Offer feedback...	
Go through...	
Explain...	
Show PowerPoint	

These objectives should be examined per audience group. You might ask managers to do something totally different from the marketing staff. If you can't find a measurable objective for each audience group, you should seriously examine whether they should be in the audience. If you have nothing for them, why should they come?

Determine the What (Finally!)

It's only after we answer the Why and the Who and are clear on Objectives that we can address the What. This bothers many people, because the What is where they are used to starting, not finishing. (Let's jump in and start hashing out what we're going to say!) But creating content before we identify the motivations that exist in the room and the needs of the audience is dangerous. We're likely to miss the audience's purpose entirely and will also probably bore them in the process.

At this point in the process, it's time to gather all the material that applies to what we've discovered about needs of the audience. Stories, facts, data, charts, graphs, pictures, exercises, lists, multimedia, quizzes, games, role plays, humor, quotes, case studies, videos. Bring it all. We'll need it as we step into the Essential.

Find the Essential

Once we've gone through Empathy, the next step in the content development process is completed comparatively quickly. We need to determine what is Essential.

Your Presentation in One Sentence

Essential is what must be in your presentation if everything else falls away. It is absolutely necessary and indispensable. Essential usually satisfies the statement, *"If you don't remember anything else I say, remember this."*

ESSENTIAL:
Absolutely
necessary;
indispensable.

At first glance, this seems easy. But I've had only one client who could answer my request of *"Give me your entire presentation summed up in one sentence"* on the first try. It is not easy. Simple, yes. Easy, no.

The problem with creating the Essential is what the Heath brothers, in their best-selling book *Made to Stick*, call the "Curse of Knowledge." *You* know what you're talking about. The *audience* likely does *not* know, and they don't know what they don't know. If you give two sentences without context or emphasis, the audience has no idea which is more important. And a rambling, detailed, exposition of your knowledge is not likely to help them much.

The Curse of Knowledge is a struggle in every communication environment. You can't remember what it's like to be a teenager, and your son rolls his eyes at your parental help. You can't remember what it's like to be a new employee, and your onboarding process is confusing and boring. You can't remember what it was like to be confused by the columns of numbers in the budget, so your explanations confound those who are about to make the purchasing decisions.

In order to find this essential sentence, lean on your previous Empathy work. As you examine your research on what your audience wants to know, needs to know, and doesn't know, you will find similarities and key elements that need to be covered. Knowing their pains, their attitudes, and their questions will give you motivation for providing a solution.

The work is in thinking. Iterating. Contemplating. Asking. But the result—an essential one-sentence thesis—provides the framework that will drive everything else you cover.

Here are some examples of essential messages from some of my keynotes and classes:

- Anyone can learn to be a great presenter.
- Successful communication is Simpler, Shorter, and Slower.
- A great communicator lives in the intersection of the Conduit, the Content, and the Connection.
- Modern business tools are ruining productivity.

The result of failing to determine the Essential is a presentation that is longer than it needs to be, more complex than it needs to be, and ultimately won't be remembered by the audience. Everyone in the audience should walk out repeating the same essential message. How they apply it will vary, of course, but the essential message should be as plain as day.

Develop Structure

Once we know what our essential message is—that one-sentence summary we want our audience to repeat, we expand on it. We put a structure in place that supports our assertion and helps our audience follow our train of thought. This structure also provides a framework for all the material we gathered in the What process.

Structure needn't be any extravagant format. This book (and everything we teach) is based on the simple belief that *"Anyone can learn to speak effectively."* Then we explain Conduit, Content, and Connection. Steve Jobs sold the iPhone as *"an iPod, a phone, and an Internet communicator...[in] one device."* Jim Valvano's ESPY speech had three main points: *"Laugh. Think. Cry. Every day."* My keynote for great communicators is built around *"Simpler. Shorter. Slower."*

The idea behind your structure should be that the audience could take notes if they wanted to and that they could repeat the core structure when asked. The points can't be tongue-twisters. You can't use words only experts know. Refine and shorten your structure until it makes sense and can be repeated by anyone. Simple. Memorable. Repeatable.

Sample Structures

You don't have to work hard to find a great structure for your presentation. There are many good ideas and you need only pick one. The following table offers some samples to get you started.

Structure	Example
Time Abraham Lincoln frequently used time to structure his speeches.	The Gettysburg Address: past, present, future. Four score and seven years ago... Now we are engaged... The world will little note, nor long remember...
Alliteration Starting your key concepts with the same letter.	Three Cs: Conduit. Content. Connection. I'm teaching you to be a "Con" man (woman).
Acronym Using your key concepts to spell a word.	EAT: At networking events, I use the acronym EAT to describe myself. It helps new connections remember me. I love to EAT: to **E**XPERIENCE life, not watch it; to **A**NALYZE (everything!); and to **T**EACH, which is what I was created to do.
Questions Answer the pressing questions on the audience's mind.	Why? Who? What? This was the structure for our Content section, and it can be extended to almost any business setting.
Ordered List This method orders, draws attention, and creates suspense.	David Letterman's Top Ten List How about "Top Ten Reasons to Become a Better Speaker!"?
Position When your topic is partitioned.	Multi-tier architecture: When I taught technical audiences about multi-server installations, I put posters on the wall to represent each computer setup. As I talked about the application server, the web server, the client, and the metadata server, I would walk to each poster for emphasis.
Pro vs. Con or **Compare and Contrast** Line up facts in a classic good vs. evil showdown.	Apple vs. PC: The humorous commercials (check YouTube) showed a stark difference between two opposing viewpoints. This approach can also be used when comparing purchase options for a sales associate.

Same Essential, Same Structure, Adjusted for Time

If you ask me in an elevator what I do, I'll say something like, *"I get normal people to speak articulately."* Ask me the secret to public speaking and I'll respond, *"Great communicators live in the intersection of a speaker's Conduit—the skills they use to deliver their message; their Content—the material and organization their audience* can digest; and a Connection—the relationship they create with their audience." Ten seconds, tops. Ding! You're off at the next floor.

If you've got $10 and a few hours, buy my book. (Better yet, buy two and give one to a friend!)

But if you have a team of 100 (and the budget to train them all), I've got workshops ranging from two hours to a week that will give your employees an experience they'll never forget, and we can change their behavior (and their lives!). Even then you won't get all the material I've uncovered about presenting well.

No matter what venue we're in or how much time we have, my essential message remains: *A great communicator lives in the intersection of the Conduit, the Content, and the Connection—and anyone can become a great communicator.* I match the length of my content to the time available.

Content is Not Linear

As you consider your content and the structure for it, consider the idea that your content is not linear. *Linear* means "in a straight line," and in the context of content, it means that one thing follows another. One thing does follow another, of course, when you are actually speaking. But viewing your presentation as a series of sentences or points can lead to disaster when time is shortened or anything goes wrong. You suddenly rush to squeeze in every idea or sentence. You find yourself saying, *"Oops, I'm going to have to skip this whole section."* PowerPoint exacerbates the problem, making you believe that your presentation is a series of slides that are numbered sequentially.

Instead, view your presentation hierarchically. Start with the main point—one sentence that takes twenty seconds. Then expand that into three supporting points—maybe a full minute now. If you are short on time, go with the quick version; when not in a rush, use all three points.

Take this book, for example. You may think since it is delivered on numbered pages (or perhaps numbered e-book 'turns'), it is linear. One thought follows another. But the writing process and the way the book was created were an entirely different matter. Even though you probably are reading the book in order, your brain is filling in gaps and connecting to other ideas, experiences, and personal stories. You read linearly; you understand modularly.

I set up front matter, to establish your interest and make the connection. I expanded our model of Conduit, Content, and Connection while defining each and outlining the Presentation Sins of each element. Within each of those sections, I have multiple structures as well: Control, Energy, Logistics. Empathy, Essential, Entertaining, Why? Who? What? And so on. Once the structure is set, all I have to do is carve out the time to fill in the details.

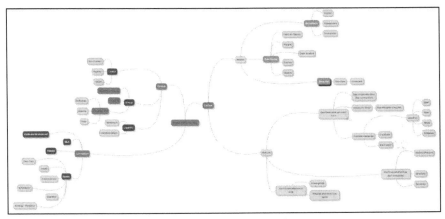

Non-linear Mind Map of This Book's Content

How much information you share in a presentation is bound only by the time and interest of your audience. The essential message stays the same. The structure stays the same. The amount of content included in the structure is what changes. We'll talk about that more when we reach Entertaining, but first...

A Reality Check

It's at this point of the process I like to stop and do what I call a Reality Check. Are we missing anything that would cause our audience to disconnect or that might offend them to the point they would no longer accept what we are trying to say? Because we are not the audience and we live under the Curse of Knowledge, this pause is critical to avoid calamity.

As before, we should do this check for each audience group. Some in your audience may say, *"All right! Let's do it!"* And others may be asking, *"What in the world is he talking about?"* Others might need more information to be won over.

Receptivity

The first stop on the Reality Check is the audience's receptivity to what you are asking them to do. If the audience members are typical, most decisions through four stages:
1. Awareness,
2. Understanding,
3. Acceptance, and
4. Commitment.

Awareness is knowing that there are options. You can't sell me a car in its luxury trim line without my knowing such a trim line exists. You don't marry someone you don't know. You don't accept a job you aren't aware of.

The first step in the process to gain the audience's action is to make them aware. The boss may not know the options. The defense may not know the opponent's strategy. You may need to introduce the problems, situations, or product to the audience to create awareness.

Once we are Aware, we seek **Understanding**. What are the facts, figures, details, and ramifications? Price, time, horsepower, color, power consumption, longevity, blocking scheme, pass route, location, and carbon footprint. We want to know the facts.

This is where experts love to talk. Give all the facts. Expand on the details. Leave no stone unturned. But what if the audience already knows the facts? You're communicating at a level they don't need. It's likely to bore them. Or what if you start explaining details but they don't know what you're talking about? Again, a disconnect.

The first two steps—Awareness and Understanding—often can be accomplished without interaction or a presentation. I can find every car and every option Honda sells at www.hondacars.com. I don't need a salesperson. I can read business books in the Amazon library and know everything there is to know about leadership. But that may not make me a good manager or leader, and it certainly won't get me a new car.

The third step—**Acceptance**—is where we begin to examine our relationship to the idea, product, or service being offered. Will it work for *me*?

There are a million variables at work here, and you as a presenter may not know any of them. Ever. You may have a great girlfriend, but you break up with the line, *"It's not you, it's me."* Your friends, parents, and mentor all thought she was the one, but the relationship didn't work for *you*. The house is affordable, in a great location, and has all the items on your checklist. The realtor is convinced he has the sale, and your best friend is encouraging you to sign the papers. However you can't, and you don't.

As a presenter, getting someone to Acceptance is hard. There are emotions and facts and history and hang-ups and peer pressure and image to contend with. You can do your best and still may lose the Acceptance battle. Ultimately, we give reasons in Understanding but leave the audience to decide in Acceptance.

The last step is **Commitment**. You accept the proposal (and the ring). You sign the contract. You agree to lead your team on the project. Commitment has a date and time and parameters for success. We're "all in."

But as a communicator, this stage is again problematic. The audience can know the product or idea exists. They can know all the facts. And they still might not act, purchase, or choose. There are a million reasons why. You might be the best candidate; they know all about you, they accept that you would do a great job, but you're not the nephew of the owner. You may have the best business strategy and everyone nods and seems to agree, but the boss doesn't tolerate risk or is a jerk. Sorry.

The Reality Check exists to make sure you are communicating on the right level and your approach is appropriate to the mindset in the room.

Interpersonal Dynamics

The next stop on our Reality Check is to figure out how the people in the room relate. Is there a 900-pound gorilla—someone who always gets his way? Is there a champion who will love and defend you no matter what? Is there an antagonist who will be against the idea no matter how valid the proposal? Is there an elephant in the room that needs to be addressed?

Once, without doing the proper investigation first, I let a manager talk me into allowing his subordinates to attend a presentation workshop with him. This manager was intolerable. He didn't let his people speak. They were scared of him. They never offered their opinions. It was one of the worst classes I've ever taught. All because the guy signing the check was a bully (and I didn't do my homework to know that).

Demographics

I was teaching a college class a few years ago and mentioned the Space Shuttle *Challenger* explosion. A kid piped up and said, *"That was before I was born."* I suddenly felt very, very old. And I made a mental note to use the *Challenger* example primarily with middle-age audiences. I wouldn't pull out my parenting stories for the college crowd either. I wouldn't discuss dating in a business context, or business ownership to a group of employees. It's called knowing your audience. It's another Reality Check you need to perform for each audience subgroup.

What are the ages in the subgroups? Genders? Nationalities? Religions (you may not discuss religion, but if you mention something offensive, ranging from drinking alcohol to activities during a holy time of year, you could easily offend someone). Political views?

How do your audience groups learn? Engineers want data and explanations. Executives usually want to hear about results. Salespeople may want interactive and involved learning experiences. Know what will work for your audience.

It's worth asking these questions to make sure you vet all your examples against your demographic.

The Competition

I once was teaching a sales group and noticed they were extremely distracted. It's not unusual for individuals to sneak peeks at their cell phones during class, but this was an exceptionally distracted bunch. I finally broached the subject head on. *"What's so important on your phones?"* Since I wasn't calling out a single person, I felt safe with the query. *"Our quarterly numbers are coming out this morning."* Ah. Their bonuses and raises were hinging on an email. They weren't too interested in the finer points of gesturing.

I got them to agree that checking emails during class wouldn't change the report. I'd give them plenty of time during breaks, and I'd lead the conga line if the news was good. But we needed to press on with our class. They laughed, relaxed, and we got on with it. Oh, and the news was good.

Your audience always has something to divert their attention. The rise of cell phones has only made it tougher on presenters. At the core we must ask, *"Is what you are saying more interesting to them than what they could be reading on their phone?"* If the answer is no, then you are fighting a losing battle.

I don't try to schedule classes during the NCAA basketball or local conference tournaments (clients sometimes schedule them for me, and I warn them of the risk!). I don't like Friday afternoons (and students don't like being in class Friday afternoons). I don't like giving keynotes before lunch (the audience wants to eat). I avoid the first (and last) day of school. The calendar is limiting to an independent training consultant!

But there could be a million other interesting distractions in your audience's head. The good: waiting for news, the prospect of an exciting weekend, a new love interest, a new job or hobby. The bad: a doctor's prognosis, a failed relationship, frustration with work, a thyroid problem.

You need to either be more interesting than the audience's distractions or be willing to share their mind.

The Decision Process

Since we're going to make an "ask" (some call to action) as part of our presentation, we need to know how the audience can answer our request. How will the decision be made?

I had a healthy debate with a sales rep once who declared her objective was to ask her audience to buy her company's product. Since her product cost over $10 *million*, it was quite an ask! We dove into who would be in the room and who could sign the check (not many people can sign an eight-digit check!). Turns out the decision maker would not be present. If the decision maker isn't present, you can't ask the listener to buy (and that's why I never take my wife with me on the first visit to a car lot!). She got defensive, and even asked haughtily if I had ever managed to get a meeting with the CEO of a Fortune 100 company. It doesn't matter. If the buyer isn't present, you don't ask for the purchase.

She was convinced that "Buy" was her action. Her sales trainer had beat into her to ask for the contract. But a Reality Check would reveal that the client's process makes that a bad ask. Instead, she should ask the attendees to *influence* the buyer.

What people, processes, and principles are at play? Who are the decision makers? How will they make a decision? If they claim they'll go to their board, then you must find out what the board will do. Is it a simple democratic vote? Does the Chair wield the power? Will they put it out for bid (the government will)? Additionally, is the decision to be based on cost, ease, comfort, reliability, relationship, or some other factors? Those answers will help drive your presentation to where it needs to go.

Expectations

I had finished teaching a class and was reading the evaluations. On one, the class and the instructor (me) got the highest marks possible—six points on a six-point scale. Except for one question: *"How well did this course meet your expectations?"* That got a three. Hunh? You say I'm a great instructor, you thought it was worth your time, the materials and content were excellent, but the course didn't meet your expectations. Those must have been some lofty expectations!

It's a key lesson in presenting to a group: your audience arrives with expectations. Since everyone has been to a bad presentation, they come wondering if this is worth their time, but they may also have one particular story they want to hear, or one fact they need to know, or one assurance they need to have. If you don't deliver, you can expect their disappointment and perhaps even animosity.

What is the *one* nugget they came expecting to hear? It's worth a Reality Check to find out.

Do Your Research

You might not know the answers to the questions in our Reality Check. That's OK. Go find out. Ask the meeting chair, the event host, the planner, the boss, or someone who plans to attend. You can almost always find out what you need to know with the right query. If you are going in blind, you might do an interactive query at the outset to find out the answers in the live environment (though recognize it is risky—you have to know what to do with the answers and when to stop asking questions!). If you have limited time and still have no idea what to expect from your audience, use wisdom and experience to aim for the most likely outcome. If you are still in the dark, hope for the best; expect the worst.

Knowing your audience before you go will increase the likelihood of a successful presentation, both in your eyes and in the eyes and hearts of your audience.

Make It Entertaining

As presenters we've gotten to know our audience as best we can through Empathy. We've discovered what we wish to accomplish. We've put an Essential one-sentence message together and a simple structure to expand to our audience. Now the fun begins.

We need to make our content Entertaining.

ENTERTAIN:

To hold the attention of pleasantly or agreeably; to admit into the mind; consider; to maintain or keep up.

When I'm teaching highly technical audiences about Entertaining, you can almost feel the tension fill the room. *"I'm not here to be funny."* Or *"This is about technical details, not a stage show."* Or *"I can be as entertaining as I want, but if they don't BUY, it doesn't matter.*" Like all the other words we've used in this book, *entertain* deserves a look in the dictionary. *Entertain*: to hold the attention of pleasantly or agreeably; to admit into the mind; consider; to hold in the mind; cherish; to maintain or keep up.

If I had opened this section by telling you that we are going to develop content that would will agreeably hold your audience's attention, that they will consider what you have to say and even adopt your main ideas, and that they'll be able to follow or keep up with you as you speak, then you'd be fully on board.

I just did that: you need to *entertain* your audience, in the truest sense of the word. This means you will never bore your audience, and you will meet *their* presentation needs, not yours. Remember: this is about them, not you. Rule #1.

Brainstorm Content Possibilities

To begin figuring out how to "entertain" the audience, we ask clients/students to bring every story, fact, graph, chart, case study, activity, video, sound clip, quiz, game, quote, picture, data table, and reference they can find relevant to their topic. They are usually experts, so there is no shortage of material.

Will we use all the material? Not likely. We'll assess to see where it fits into the context of our essential structure (if it does). Then we have to look at the time available to us.

Fill the Structure Using the Speaker Grid

Assuming you know your topic, crafting your presentation becomes a simple outline made up of building blocks of entertaining content. Usually, you have more information that you have time to share. This is where we let our audience (and our host) tell us what we can include.

Even when I'm giving a speech again, I like to go through the building blocks to make sure each one matches the style of the audience, the time I'm allotted, and the tenor of the presentation.

I use a spreadsheet to develop speeches. Really. It's called the Speaker Grid, and I teach it to my clients too. I put the essential message across the top with the essential structure in a column down the left side. Then I expand the outline into columns. Each column offers supporting points for the main ideas. I'm very partial to threes, although there is no law that says it has to be threes. Each row should follow the simple, memorable, repeatable rubric. Ideally, this would be the level of detail I could expect an audience to repeat.

For the MillsWyck Communications training I do (and for this book), my 3x3 Speaker Grid looks like this:

Essential Message: **Anyone Can Be an Effective Speaker**			
Main Idea 1: **Conduit**	Support 1a: **Control**	Support 1b: **Energy**	Support 1c: **Logistics**
Main Idea 2: **Content**	Support 2a: **Empathy**	Support 2b: **Essential**	Support 2c: **Entertaining**
Main Idea 3: **Connection**	Support 3a: **Engagement**	Support 3b: **Visuals**	Support 3c: **Q&A**

This is where my entertaining content has a home. Every detail, fact, story, example, exercise, movie clip, and sound bite needs to land somewhere in this grid. If you add a repeatable structure to each cell of the Speaker Grid, it becomes *really* easy for the audience to follow (and for you to remember!).

For instance, in our live workshops we cover the following three questions for each of the Conduit skills:

1. What does it do for the audience?

2. What does it do for the speaker?

3. What technique is effective?

By the time we hit skill number three (facial expressions), the audience knows what's coming, and the dialog and interaction level is high. If they ever need to recreate the learning from class, they've got a framework to recall, and if they don't, a short email to me will get the answer.

This also makes it easy to add new material. When I recently got a tip from a student about how to make your smile better (push your tongue against your upper palate, right behind your teeth), I asked myself, *"Where does it fit in?"* Smiling is part of facial expressions, which is an Energy skill. I added one more tip to that cell.

If you spend the time to create a structure for your talk, then filling out the rest is a relatively quick process. After all, you are the expert, so expanding details should not be the problem.

You'll find that your biggest decisions are about what *doesn't* belong, because anything that does belong will have a home. What guides you in determining which content belongs and which doesn't? The Empathy step you went through earlier. Is the content meaningful to the audience? Do you have time to cover it? *"Yes"* and it's in. *"No"* and you leave it out.

Remembering Your Content: Using Notes

In an ideal world we would all have photographic memories that quickly recalled our presentation information and sized it to fit our time parameters. Some experienced speakers—often professionals who give the same speech again and again—can present for a hour without breaking eye contact with the audience. The rest of us typically need notes to remind us what to say.

There are any number of note forms you can use: notecards, bullets on a piece of paper, a teleprompter (for times you are required to read word for word). Find and use a system that works for YOU.

I use the Speaker Grid. For speeches with brand new content, I might also have a few pages of supporting details in case I need them. For speeches where I'm familiar with the content but not completely confident in my memory, I might have a few bullets in each box of the grid. For speeches I have given many times, my grid might be as simple as the example above—one word per box. I have told a story about the Gettysburg Address so many times, I have one word in my notes: *Gettysburg*. I only need to glance at the clock to remind myself what detail level and interaction level to use before I begin with *"On November 19th, 1863..."* I have a one-minute version, and can work a training class on the subject for fifteen minutes. Same structure. Same point. (The point, by the way, is that a shorter speech is more likely to be remembered than a longer one is.)

Regardless of what notes method you use, remember that when you consult your notes, you should pause (in other words, be silent). Once you've refreshed your memory, reset, make eye contact with the audience, and continue.

As you become more familiar with your content, you'll need fewer prompts. The most common mistake speakers tend to make with notes is having too many of them. Have you ever found yourself in the middle of a presentation, pausing to look at your notes and realizing you have to flip five pages to catch up to where you are? That's a good indicator you didn't need those notes—at least not to that detail level.

And now, create the Visuals (Finally!)

It's at this point—the END of content development—that we begin to think about slides. We know everything the audience needs to hear. We have our points in a concise form and expanded to the depth the audience needs. If we decide that visuals would enhance the presentation, we include them, but only if that's the case. *Visuals are a purposeful decision, not a default.*

Visuals may not even be needed. We teach our two-day Conduit workshops and don't use PowerPoint once. I give many of my inspirational keynotes for 45-90 minutes and never turn on a projector. But when I taught technical training, visuals made concepts easier to understand; demos helped concepts sink in; and exercises were worth ten hours of lecture.

When it helps, and *only when it helps,* use visuals. But develop them AFTER you know your message in its entirety.

The easiest visuals are the ones that support the message structure. You might have three visuals for each of your key points of structure. Then you might have one each for the supporting subpoints. A story might be better told with a picture, and the data might be clearer with a graph, but note we're adding visuals to support an *existing* message, not creating a message in the visual tool. There's a big difference, and the audience will appreciate it. More on visuals later…

Variations on a Theme

This content development method shines when it's time to repurpose previous content. If you have to give the same (or similar) message to another audience, you can reduce your prep time and customize your content easily for different groups and varying time slots. Once you understand the basic audience groups, finding Empathy and conducting a Reality Check are quick, the Essential is the same, and the Entertaining process gets easier every time you do it. I can frequently write speeches in a half hour by reusing modules and audience analysis. If I were starting from scratch, it would take days. Or weeks.

Changing the length of your presentation is as simple as changing the detail level of your entertainment. To shorten the time, you might eliminate a group exercise or toss out a story. To increase the time, you might ask someone to join you on stage to use as an example or help you teach.

I worked with a client who was leading two introductory meetings at her new job: one with the staff and one with the non-profit board that hired her. We crafted the core message of her introduction, which included her vision for the organization and how she fit in. We expanded it for each audience and as time would allow (one was five minutes, the other fifteen minutes). The two presentations were easier to prepare because the essential message stayed the same. In the future when a staff member comes to her with questions or issues, she can return to that core message, likely in even further expanded form. There's no reason to reinvent the wheel.

If you are an organizational leader, your vision isn't likely to change in the short term. Only the stories and the details change as you meet throughout the year recasting and reaffirming the vision with your team. Once you find the essential message, it becomes easy to stay on point and develop supporting material.

This expandable approach also works when the three speakers before you all ran over their allotted time during their portion of the meeting and your boss says you have five minutes instead of fifteen. Your core message *does not change*. Only the depth (and thus, time) changes.

Core Content Sins

Now that we've gone through the content development process, let's take a look at places presenters commonly trip up with content. In many cases, you'll find that more than one of the Es (Empathy, Essential, Entertainment) applies.

SIN: Not Highlighting What's Important

At the end of a group presentation, a hand went up. The question was vague but hinting at wanting the bottom line. The asker began his thoughts, *"Would it be safe to say that you think we should..."*

The presenter shook his head and responded with a sneer, *"That was sorta the point of my presentation."* I chuckled to myself. Sorta the point, but apparently *not* the point, or the listener wouldn't have had to ask or assume.

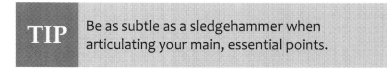

TIP Be as subtle as a sledgehammer when articulating your main, essential points.

SIN: Presenting What Isn't Important

I witnessed a tag team of first-time presenters who, in their haste to make things entertaining, had produced a slideshow of pictures from the project they were introducing and a home-made rap video about the project. It was cute. Almost. OK, it was tolerable. But the video was two minutes, there were at least ten slides of pictures, their examples were repetitive (the concept itself was trivial to understand in the first place). When a question was allowed to run amok and meeting time ran short, the presentation came to a conclusion with the speakers looking at one another and shrugging with the comment, *"Well, we didn't get to the main points of our presentation, but we hope you enjoyed it and got a feel for what we're about."*

In journalism, this is known as "burying the lede." Hoping your audience gets a feel for what you are saying is not a communication strategy. It's a sign of a poorly planned talk whose content is not designed for the audience's best interest.

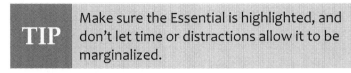

TIP Make sure the Essential is highlighted, and don't let time or distractions allow it to be marginalized.

SIN: Presenting Irrelevant Information

I was working a client through the content development process. She was an insurance expert who consulted with small and medium businesses on their group health plans. After months of work and details, the company would invite her to tell the employees about their new health care plan options. It would inevitably be a packed house (people care about their health and their money!). She came to me because she knew she was boring them. We got to her essential message pretty fast: *"Your company has created a great health plan for you; you and your family are going to be taken care of."* She had wonderful structure and supporting content for what the employees needed to do:

- What they **HAVE** to do
- What they **SHOULD** do
- Immediate **ACTION**

If you're paying attention, you'll note that forms the very nice acronym of "HSA," which also was the type of new plan their employees were moving to. Catchy, huh?!

We added supporting categories. Then we had to fill out the presentation. I asked her to catalog all the stories, facts, figures, and forms she shared. I asked her to put all her "entertainment" items into one of the boxes of the Speaker Grid. She came to a startling discovery.

She had seventeen items in her previous presentation. Only two were put in her Speaker Grid. The other fifteen were justification for her decision—a decision that was already made and which no one in the audience could change. Most of her existing presentation had *nothing* to do with what the audience cared about.

We added some stories and data that supported her main points. The presentation went from two hours (yikes!) to fifteen minutes. She called me after the first one to say the client was thrilled and the audience didn't look bored. Success!

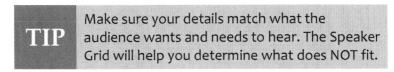

TIP Make sure your details match what the audience wants and needs to hear. The Speaker Grid will help you determine what does NOT fit.

SIN: Failing to Verify Facts

The speaker being introduced was not only an accomplished author but also had his own radio show. The introducer started with *"I'm so thrilled to have the opportunity to introduce my good friend and hero, Joe, today."* Then he moved to the book, apparently making up its reach with the comment *"It's sold something like...a million copies!"* Then, he highlighted the radio show with an uncertain, *"And I think you can hear him speak on local radio 105.7 at... uh, I think it's at nine o'clock, but I'm not sure."* The audience was left thinking that this person sure didn't know much about his hero.

If a fact is to be quoted or used or is instrumental in making a point, it should be researched and used correctly. While it's certainly preferable to drop an "I think" when not confident in quoting a fact (rather than confidently misstating it!), things that are easily found should be researched and found. (Hint: Google is your friend!) If an audience realizes that a speaker didn't take twenty seconds to research a fact, the speakers' credibility is drawn into question.

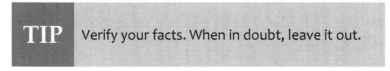

TIP Verify your facts. When in doubt, leave it out.

SIN: Plagiarism? Or Flattery?

A client came to me for a review of his presentation. It contained a veritable Who's Who of pop culture. He had video snippets, cartoons, references to movie lines, stories, and punch lines that I (and everyone else) knew were not his originally. When I asked him about it, he replied, *"Hey, imitation is the highest form of flattery. And they always get a laugh. People love it! I don't see anything wrong with it."*

He may be right, but if the only skill you're known for is using other people's material, your name better be Weird Al Yankovic. You also need a legal team to clear the way for your material.

I had an embarrassing moment after re-using a one-liner. I had heard a zinger that got a big laugh and decided to use it in a class I was teaching. As I hit the punch line, several folks gave a token laugh and one person blurted out disappointedly, *"That came from Seinfeld."* Since I wasn't a fan of the show, I had no idea where the quip came from, and I'm sure the look on my face and whatever stumbled out of my mouth dragged my humor credibility through the mud. I had not prepared for that response, hadn't researched the quote, and got shown up on the stage.

 TIP Always be able to cite your sources. If you're "re-purposing" another's content, you'd better have permission and reference its origin.

NOTEWORTHY: Intellectual Property

Disclaimer: I'm not a lawyer, and I don't play one on TV. But you can be sued for using material you do not have the right to use. Just because you found it on the Internet does not make it fair game, especially in a commercial context. There is a "fair use" clause, and thirty minutes and a Google search should convince you that those of us who are not attorneys don't have a clue what the real law says. When in doubt, leave it out.

SIN: Giving Less than You Promised

I watched a personal improvement coach deliver a message titled *"Seven ways to...[something or other]."* In his live presentation, he gave three ways to "something or other." When an audience member asked him about the complete list, he said we'd have to buy his book to get the other four.

He over-promised and under-delivered. (W-aaa-yy undelivered.)

 TIP Instead of promising seven and giving four, promise seven and give ten. Or promise four and give seven. Even if you can't go into depth on each item, simply listing them keeps your promise to the audience.

SIN: Not Knowing Your Audience

At an extremely popular technical conference (4000+ attendees), the first presentation of the day started before breakfast. Despite the early hour, it still drew 2500 attendees. First, the chief technical officer of the sponsoring company gave his take on the future of the company's products. After his short presentation, he introduced a motivational speaker who was to speak on "innovation."

She opened with *"After listening to that, I just realized I have no idea what you people do."* Then she launched into her 45-minute keynote. Only no one was listening. Virtually everyone was on their phone, laptop, or tablet. Some slept.

Perhaps the early hour and the social activities the night before contributed to the (lack of) response. But the #1 reason the audience was MIA was that the speaker failed on the most basic level: she disrespected the audience. She may as well have said, *"I did not consider you worthy of investigation, and spent no time trying to figure out what you do. I have a canned presentation that I am going to give no matter who you are or what you are interested in."*

Do your research ahead of time so you can find common ground with your audience.

SIN: Assuming the Audience Thinks Like You Do

In the Southern U.S., where I've lived since I was an infant, if you said you didn't know barbeque came from a pig, the response might be, *"Y'all ain't from 'round here, is ye?"* (I know I promised I wouldn't talk about religion, and I failed you on that point: BBQ is about as fervent a religious conviction as one can have, but I use it for illustrative purposes only and will not try to win you over to one side or the other! I recognize barbeque in other parts of the country varies in style, animal, and fervor.)

People who aren't like the speaker are "y'all." You all.

The mindset of "y'all" is a critical sin for the presenter. Your audience members are NOT uniform. They are individuals, with individual needs, hopes, perspectives, and attention spans.

To uphold Rule #1 (It's not about you), you should research your audience—ahead of time.

 Don't assume your audience thinks, acts, or behaves the same way you do. Find Empathy and key differences ahead of time.

SIN: Misjudging the Audience's Receptivity Level

A company I worked for was known for its great benefits. Only one benefit consistently got complaints—the pension plan. Because the company had been formed by young professionals with a long work life ahead of them, establishing a robust pension plan wasn't a priority. The biggest complaint people had was the amount of time you needed to be at the company and the age you had to reach before the retirement package would kick in.

One January 21st, the entire company received an email. It began, *"Effective January 1..."* (as in, *three weeks ago*). The email went on to say that the formula used to compute an employee's retirement date had changed, as had some of the benefits. Because of that policy change (announced three weeks after it became effective, via email), my retirement age moved seventeen years. SEVENTEEN. YEARS. I knew at least one person who had been planning to retire the year the email came out, but now was ineligible to retire for TEN MORE YEARS.

Let me be clear: the problem was not the decision itself. The company management did what they believed to be best for the company, and I have to believe they did it with their eyes wide open and all pertinent information considered, but the communication was *horrendous*. They communicated from a position of commitment (It's done!), and the audience was not even aware a change was coming (*"You're thinking about changing the retirement policy?"*). While it is possible to function this way, if you're trying to create good will, then handing out ultimatums and decisions with no background is not an effective way to communicate.

If you want input, ask for it. If you want acceptance, explain (on the audience's terms). If you know the audience won't like what is being communicated, acknowledge that. Then, as part of telling the audience what they don't want to hear, explain your motivation and the positive end result you ultimately expect.

 TIP Find out the audience receptivity level before you propose or inform, especially on potentially controversial topics.

SIN: Not Testing Your Material

In my son's youth football league, the head coach had an unfortunate schedule conflict for our team's biggest game of the year. We knew team we were about to face had one player for whom we had no answer. The head coach had prepared a contingency in case our regular stock of plays didn't work. But weather cancellations had resulted in our having no chance to practice the week leading up to the game. We had only a diagram via email showing us how to execute the game plan.

On game day the well-meaning (and short-straw) volunteer assistant who drew the task of managing the team that day introduced a new play that he felt would counteract the other team's powerhouse kid and give us a chance to win. I'm convinced it would have worked IF...we'd had a chance to practice it, but putting in a new play for ten-year-olds thirty minutes before kickoff is like tossing a new story into the middle of your keynote as you drive to the facility to speak. It doesn't work.

 Don't go into the biggest opportunity you've ever had and try something new without testing it first.

The Open Block

We stated that the tell 'em, tell 'em, tell 'em method is good for reinforcement. Now let's look at what else needs to be added to get attention and action from an adult audience. Once we've created the core content for our presentation, it's time to start bookending it.

Before we get to our core content, there has to be a set-up, so we begin with the Open Block, which includes:

- Getting the audience's **attention**
- Giving them a **reason to listen**, and
- **Removing any obstacles** that may distract them.

If we were to add the Open Block to our speaker's grid, it would look like this (first row, in bold):

Essential Message: Anyone Can Be an Effective Speaker			
Open Block	**Attention**	**Reason to Listen**	**Remove Obstacles**
Main Idea 1: Conduit	Support 1a: Control	Support 1b: Energy	Support 1c: Logistics
Main Idea 2: Content	Support 2a: Empathy	Support 2b: Essential	Support 2c: Entertaining
Main Idea 3: Connection	Support 3a: Engagement	Support 3b: Visuals	Support 3c: Q&A

Get Their Attention

Dale Carnegie says you should have something interesting to say from the very first word. Not from the first minute. Not from the first idea. From the first *word*.

Ways to start with "something interesting" from the first word include:

- Telling a **story**
- Offering an amazing **fact**
- **Quoting** a famous (or not so famous) person on the topic of the day
- Connecting a current **event** happening locally or globally to a problem your audience faces
- Asking a **question**

The key to choosing your attention-getting opener is to look at your essential content (see prior sections). Based on your main point, choose one of these methods that naturally leads to that point.

A Story

I've created a business opener based on what I've learned from children's stories. (Disney has made a fortune off this technique, so it must work.) It's the fairy tale.

Open with the **setting**. *"Once upon a time..."* probably won't work well for the board meeting, so change it up to *"We find ourselves facing..."* (or any variant that works for you). Tell the audience where we are.

Next up in a fairy tale is the **conflict**. Why won't the princess get the prince? Why aren't our sales rising as we want? Why don't we have more self-discipline?

Then the story (in this case, your presentation) should fill in the **resolution**. I like to set this up with a question. *"How can we raise revenue without increasing staff?"*

This takes little preparation and sounds amazingly structured and well thought-out. Templates like this are wonderful ways to make speaking easy. See the Connection chapter for more on storytelling.

A Fact

Did you know the world's fastest animal, the cheetah, can run 75 mph? Oooh. Aaaah. And *"So what?"*

Data and facts are often used as de facto proof for a speaker's points, but—and this pains me to say as a former math teacher— data and facts are meaningless. We live in the information age. If I want data and facts, I need ten seconds on my phone. Wikipedia will tell me this fact about a cheetah and a whole lot more. Your quoting facts about the animal doesn't draw me. It may actually distract me by making me pull out my phone to check on you or find some random web page listing twenty-five other fast land animals.

Instead of information, strive to deliver *insight*. Insight is valuable. Insight makes you worth listening to.

I'm not suggesting that you do away with facts and data. I use them all the time, and you should too. However, when using facts and data, there are three insights you need to share and confirm to your audience:

1. Is it big or small?
2. Is it expected or unexpected?
3. What does it mean to the audience?

A cheetah running at 70+ miles per hour is crazy fast. It's the fastest land animal on the planet and almost three times faster than the fastest human. It's a BIG number!

But cheetahs' speed is not the asset that helps them the most. It's acceleration, their ability to change direction, and using strategy to hunt on their terms and not their prey's. If they are left to chase for long distances, they cannot do it.

Here's where we can apply the lessons of a cheetah to all sorts of audiences. For athletes, we might talk about body heat, improving acceleration, fast-twitch muscles, and form. To a business audience, we might talk about competing in arenas we can win (a cheetah is almost defenseless, so it will run rather than fight) and the value of taking care of our groups (only 10% of cheetahs survive in the wild because momma cheetah is running from predators). For an inspirational message we might find a heartwarming National Geographic clip and story. But we have to find a way to make this random fact apply to our audience.

A Quote

"The ones who are crazy enough to think they can change the world are usually the ones who do." — *Steve Jobs*

When using quotes, make sure there is a reasonable likelihood the source of the quote is either known to everyone (Mother Teresa, John Maxwell, Michael Jordan, the CEO of your company) or can be easily explained. Set the quote up, give it quickly, and move on to the connection of how the quote relates to the topic at hand.

A particularly effective method of quoting is using words from your existing audience—quoting something that has been said during your presentation. This is known as a "callback," and it's especially connective to everyone in the room, since they were present when the quote originated. Using callbacks takes the ability to think on your feet and apply to your topic and structure.

A Current Event

When I open my "Championship Speaking" keynote, I look for a story of a champion to start the talk. If the Olympics are current, I borrow a story from them. If the Scripps National Spelling Bee is on ESPN, I comment on the kids' training regimens (they make my brain hurt!). If the local high school soccer team just won the state championship, I congratulate the team and the fans. These events all tie to the speech's theme: *"Hard work pays off."*

A Question

"What is the most important decision you will make this week?" Opening with a question like this causes your audience to think, and a thinking audience will want to listen.

Asking a probing question is the shortest of all opening methods. Be sure to pause to let the audience answer in their own minds.

Give Them a Reason to Listen

Everyone has attended a bad presentation. The audience likely is wondering if yours will be bad. Let's assure them it will not.

The way to get the audience mentally ready to receive what you are about to say is to give them a promise for the exchange of their time. What will they get if they listen to you for thirty minutes? Inspiration? Motivation? All the information needed to make a decision? A headache?

State the benefit right up front, immediately after the open and with the full attention of the audience. Tell them what benefit they will receive in exchange for their time. You'll note I took the same approach at the outset of this book. After my personal story (which is likely at least a little similar to yours), I told you what you'd get out of this book and how to read it. That gives you some idea that this book is worth your time.

The reason to listen needn't be long; a few sentences is fine. However, it must address the needs and wants of the audience and give them a promise that their time is well spent.

Remove Obstacles

Once I have the audience's attention and have given them a reason to listen, I need to make sure they are at ease with how the session will proceed. I call this "removing obstacles."

The audience has three main obstacles you must remove (though there may be others):

1. **Credibility** – The information and qualifications that give you the right to stand and speak on the subject.
2. **Background** – The answer to the question, "Why are you speaking?" There has to be a reason. It may be your expertise, your position, or your desire.
3. **Logistics** – How we will handle breaks, lunch, handouts, whether the slides are posted, how many notes they should take, and what to do with their questions. Address this (very!) briefly and move on.

Once the audience members are confident of a good presentation by someone who knows how to handle the topic professionally, they can relax and listen. If you don't address these questions, you may be faced with skepticism and distraction.

Opening Sins

SIN: The "TCP" (Typical Corporate Presentation) Open

I had a friend—an extremely bright and geeky friend—get an invitation to audition for the national speaking circuit in his field. Since he recognized that he was an expert in programming computers, not in speaking, he called me. He invited me to a lunch-n-learn to watch him speak and tell him what he needed to do. I attended his dry run talk and knew immediately a few facts about this guy's chances of making the circuit.

When we debriefed the following day, I asked him to evaluate himself. *"How'd you do?"* I asked.

"It wasn't great. I know that," he replied.

"What didn't you like?" I further queried.

He responded, *"I don't know. I just felt like I lost their attention at some point, but I didn't know what to do about it."*

I smiled and, because our friendship could support it, I said, *"I disagree. You didn't lose your audience's attention. You never had it."*

Fred had begun with the "TCP" opening, *"Hi, my name is Fred, and today I'm going to talk with you about…"*

The Typical Corporate Presentation open.

The TCP open is a signal to the audience that they are about to hear information they already know or information they don't care about. The phones come out; the texting begins.

 TIP Don't open with your name and topic. Use something fun or interesting or scary that captures the audience's attention right away.

SIN: "Before we get started..."

At a day-long training class, the instructor opened with his bio, class rules, caveats, tool references, and restroom locations—all before the first page of course notes was turned. One of his comments generated a firestorm of questions that threatened to derail class.

After fifty minutes, he uttered the comment, *"Well, before we get started, I want to cover these final few things..."*

That's funny. I thought we already started—nearly an hour ago!

When you say, *"Before we get started...,"* the audience hears, *"The stuff I think is important will start in a little bit, but I'm required to (or I'm just selfish and want to) cover this less important material first. Make sure you're really tuned in later, but now you don't have to give me your full attention."*

The material that follows "Before we get started" usually falls in one of three categories:

- **Administrivia** – Facts and instructions the audience needs to know, such as when lunch will be served, program changes, location of the bathrooms, and what you should do if you have questions.
- **Fun facts or trivia** – This may concern someone in the audience, like the group birthday list, a question raised during the break, or some event like last night's ballgame.
- **Back story** – Your personal journey (or the story of how you got roped into teaching this class), which may or may not be relevant to the topic at hand.

TIP View your first words as the start of your presentation. Never demote any part of your talk to unimportant. Instead, create a "Remove Obstacles" portion of your talk.

SIN: Thanking Evvvvvveryone

"Well, I just want to thank our esteemed chair for that wonderful intro-duction. And thanks to the executive team for inviting me here today. And thanks for the wonderful program committee; their hospitality has been unbelievable. Thanks to the food service staff for the wonderful meal today. Thanks to the air conditioner repairman who got us cooled off on this hot day. Thanks to my mom for giving me the upbringing to say 'Thank You' whenever it is warranted. And thanks to my speech coach, Alan Hoffler, who gave me the skills to stand in front of you today and told me to never start a speech by listing and thanking people."

We call this the Macy's opening: it's a Thanksgiving Day Parade!

Rather than taking your audience's time with a long list of people (who I am sure are all very nice and most assuredly deserve to be thanked, so make sure you do), consider opening your presentation with something that appeals to the mind, heart, and senses of *all* your audience members.

Oh, and thank you for reading this section of the book.

TIP Before or after your presentation, offer a heartfelt handshake and kind word to thank those who have helped you. If you must say something in your presentation, work it in to your content rather than the opening.

SIN: Telling the Audience How Important You Are

A nationally-known speaker visited a local group I belong to. We met in a small, almost intimate, setting. I cannot imagine that anyone in the audience had not at least heard of this Big Wig. If they hadn't, they certainly weren't left in the dark for long.

His presentation began with a five-minute introduction read verbatim (and in a monotone voice) by the sponsor. After excruciating details of scholarly study, family activities, and a laundry list of accomplishments, a ninety-second promotional video set to rock music commenced. Almost fifteen percent of the time allotted for the speaker was promotion of him and his products (and that didn't include the books-in-the-back-of-the-room pitch at the end).

At a conference soon after, I heard another speaker introduced by an eager host who listed the speaker's accomplishments and accolades for a comparable five minutes. At the end of this amazing recitation, the speaker got up and said, *"I could listen to an introduction like that all day."* The audience laughed. *"And for a minute, I thought I was going to have to!"* The audience roared. What relief that the speaker didn't take himself as seriously as the introducer did!

There's a reason you're on the stage. You're speaking; the audience is listening. Introductions should be brief and tell the audience what THEY want to know about you. There are situations where your *bona fides* may need to be established; in that case, ask the host to make the introduction.

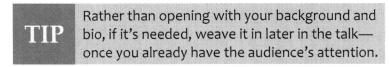

TIP: Rather than opening with your background and bio, if it's needed, weave it in later in the talk— once you already have the audience's attention.

SIN: Telling the Audience What You're Going to Cover

I went to a one-day training class where the first hour was spent on page one of the handouts under the guise of *"What we'll cover in this class."* I resisted the urge to say that we could probably finish by lunch if we started talking instead of talking about what we were going to talk about.

In the education world, I care about outcomes. What will I get from your class/seminar/workshop/tutorial? Give me those outcomes and I couldn't care less what you talk about or how long.

In the keynote/entertainment world, I want to have a great emotional experience. I don't need you to tell me the destination. Just take me with you.

In business meetings, I don't need an agenda of things to discuss. I need to know what the meeting's objective is; what are we going to accomplish? Make a decision? Great—once it's made, we're done!

In an email, this concept is called the subject line. It's not the subject paragraph.

Get to the point. Take the audience with you.

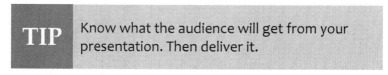

TIP Know what the audience will get from your presentation. Then deliver it.

SIN: Telling the Audience What You Will NOT Cover

In a multi-day, high-tech training class I attended, the instructor spent the entire first section of the class outlining the planned syllabus and what would be covered. However, most of the bulleted items were stated in the negative: *"We will NOT cover the installation of the product." "We will NOT cover the configuration of the product."* Since some knowledge of those topics was absolutely required to cover the things that WERE of interest, a lengthy discussion ensued about where that content stopped. That delineation actually took longer than it did to explain what we needed to know.

Nearly as bad as telling the audience what you will cover is the sin of telling the audience what you will NOT cover. If you're not going to cover it, why bring it up? Usually, this tactic comes from one of three sources:

1. **I don't want to talk about it; it's off limits.** For instance, a coach opens his press conference with, *"We will not be talking about my star player's criminal arrest today."* Anyone who brings it up can expect a rather curt reply (or no reply).

2. **I don't know enough to talk about it.** This is often the case when the speaker is not an expert in ancillary topics. He might say, *"We won't be discussing..."* which gives him an out when a question is asked.

3. **It is a can of worms we don't need to go into.** There could be any number of legitimate reasons why this is the case.

There can be situations in which it is a good idea to say what will not be covered. For example, in a technical training or conference setting if the audience must have a basic level of competence or some prerequisite knowledge to understand the material, it's safe to reiterate what will not be covered (though I'd suggest that prerequisite should be made clear in the registration materials). Even here, the exception has exceptions. What if you go to teach a class and discover NONE of the students has the prerequisites? You can say you're not going to cover them all you want, but you're wasting everyone's time unless you do.

 TIP Jump into well-structured content and leave the caveats out. You'll cover more and will likely avoid the rabbit holes.

SIN: Ignoring That Big Gray Animal Everyone Can See

I was at a firm where a new VP had been named. He was an internal candidate, but not one who was in line via the organizational chart. It was a surprise to everyone, and there was some serious doubt whether he had what it would take to lead the organization. The water cooler talk had not been kind. At his first town hall, he opened with the statement, *"I guess you're all wondering why I've been named the VP."* There were chuckles and a few eyebrows raised. He had acknowledge the #1 issue that everyone had on their mind. He went on to say, *"I thought I'd address that before we go any further. Here to tell you why is your CEO..."* The CEO gave his explanation for the hire and ended by saying, *"He's got some good ideas. I expect you to offer him your full effort and support in carrying them out."* It didn't take 30 seconds.

Had the new VP failed to address this issue, the audience would have been looking for reasons to be critical and not follow the vision. But by having their fears addressed, the employees' general tone became a positive one, and the regime change started smoothly.

 TIP If there's an elephant in the room, address it up front, not later. Don't let any audience skepticism build. Get it out in the open.

The Close Block

You've opened strong, interacted with the audience, amused them with your wry sense of humor, and clearly communicated your message. It's time for the dismount.

The Close Block consists of:

- A **summary** of your essential message,
- A **call to action**, and
- The **wrap-up**.

Putting the Close Block into our speaker grid looks like this (last row, in bold):

Essential Message: Anyone Can Be an Effective Speaker			
Open Block	Attention	Reason to Listen	Remove Obstacles
Main Idea 1: Conduit	Support 1a: Control	Support 1b: Energy	Support 1c: Logistics
Main Idea 2: Content	Support 2a: Empathy	Support 2b: Essential	Support 2c: Entertaining
Main Idea 3: Connection	Support 3a: Engagement	Support 3b: Visuals	Support 3c: Q&A
Close Block	Summarize	Call to Action	Wrap-up

Summarize Your Essential Message

Even though your core message is simple, memorable, and re-peatable, your listeners are hearing it for the first time. Marketers strive for multiple imprints to a consumer's mind (you see those commercials over and over). We should learn from them.

When you complete each of your main ideas and each supporting point, it's time to let the audience know that one thought, topic, or section is ending and another is starting. In the middle of your presentation, these are called segues. You should use them to repeat the structure to that point. For example, when teaching the Conduit, I might say, *"We've looked at driving the impression of confidence through control. We've seen that passion is observed through our energy. Now we want to drive the impression of professionalism by handling logistics."* Or at the Main idea level: *"We looked at the Conduit. We've created the Content. Now we turn our attention to the Connection."*

At the end of your presentation, don't let the opportunity pass to make sure the audience knows your core message. In training classes, I like to end every day with an interactive, *"What are you leaving with this evening that you didn't arrive with this morning?"* We have a little review session, and I don't stop until the main ideas are all on the table. Remember, your main idea satisfies the statement, *"If you don't remember anything else I say, remember..."* Say it again.

Make a Call to Action

When we were analyzing our audience, we said that our goal should be to change our world. That manifested itself in some measurable objectives. This is the time to look your audience in the eye and ask them to make that change. *"I'm asking you to support our program with a grant approval." "Please go to Amazon and submit a review for the book." "Go to our website and read about our product. Call me with questions." "Bring your decision maker to our next meeting, please."*

Some people feel uncomfortable making an "ask." Let me share a template with you that makes it smooth and appropriate for the audience. We're going for a ride in the CAR:

- **Claim** – A statement of personal experience,
- **Action** – The request, and
- **Result** – The result the action will bring.

Claim

First, we make a statement of our experience by claiming a belief or thought.

There are many phrases that work; just pick one.

- *In my experience…*
- *I believe…*
- *I think …*
- *I feel…*
- *I have found…*
- *In my opinion…*
- *I've realized…*

The reason this approach is powerful is that your claim, belief, and experience cannot be argued with. I might think you're crazy, but I cannot argue that you don't believe what you claim.

President John F. Kennedy used this approach in a budget speech before Congress in 1961 to inspire a nation to one of its greatest achievements. His claim was audacious: *"I believe that this nation should commit itself to achieving the goal, before this decade is out, of landing a man on the moon and returning him safely to the earth."* Many people thought JFK was crazy. There were LOTS of other pressing issues we could focus on, but we couldn't argue with his belief.

Action

Next, offer the action. What, exactly, are you asking the audience to do? Again, this can be phrased many ways:

- *What I would like you to do…*
- *What I'm asking you to…*
- *Would you please…*
- *Your mission, should you choose to accept it…*

JFK used this in his speech: *"I therefore ask the Congress, above and beyond the increases I have earlier requested for space activities, to provide the funds which are needed to meet the following national goals…"*

Result

Finally, give the audience the results that are linked to the action. Tell them what they'll get:

- *What you'll find…*
- *As a result…*
- *The consequences of doing (or not doing) this are…*

Again, JFK: *"No single space project in this period will be more impressive to mankind, or more important for the long-range exploration of space; and none will be so difficult or expensive to accomplish."*

CAR: Claim. Action. Result. Fill in the blanks for a straightforward call to action. It's an easy formula to generate interest and move your audience to action.

Wrap It Up

I could list several different techniques for closing your presentation, but let me give you the one simple guideline that works every time. For connection and clarity, end the way you started.

- If you open with a story, go Paul Harvey and tell "the rest of the story."
- If you open with a question, clarify the answer.
- If you open with current events, predict the future.
- If you open with a quote, end with a quote, or a modification of the original quote.

In one of my keynotes on passion, I open with a quote by Mark Twain: *"The man who can read and does not read has no advantage over the man who cannot read."* I express the ideas you've already read about passion—it has to be demonstrated, not necessarily possessed. I end with a modification to the quote: *"The man who has passion and does not show passion has no advantage over the man who has no passion."* Then I walk off the stage.

Closing Sins

SIN: Forgetting the Call to Action

An engineer friend was supporting a sales call where the prospect was asking questions such as, *"When can we have this on site?"* and *"Who would be the person installing this here?"* The engineer was shocked that the sales executive was content to let the conversation end with nothing more than a *"We'll be in touch."* My guess is this particular salesperson had a short-lived sales career.

Usually salespeople are among the best at closing, and rest of us could learn from them. We're often a lot more like the poor salesman in the example—we give impassioned information and hope for the best. But one part of the close should always be present: a call to action.

In a sales call, a call to action is asking for the business. In a meeting, it's the clarification of action items. In a speech, it's the one-two punch at the end to encourage your audience to do something, no matter how small, that will change their world.

I (the speaker) call you (the audience) to *act*.

This objective should have been uncovered in your efforts at finding Empathy. Don't abandon it as you close.

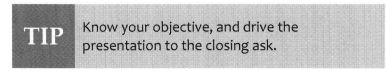

TIP   Know your objective, and drive the presentation to the closing ask.

SIN: Hawking Goods from the Stage

At an evening seminar with about a hundred hobbyists in attendance, the presenter was tasked with giving an informative presentation regarding some of the finer points of the subject they all loved and shared. These seminars were usually big social events—everyone you met was your friend, and stories abounded. These presentations were sponsored by an organization, so there was no cost to the participants except their two-hour investment of time. Midway through the program an intermission was offered for bio breaks and stretching.

As the lead-in to the break, the presenter told the audience about his new book coming out. The book had absolutely nothing to do with the seminar topic, and the "infomercial" was almost ten minutes long. The presenter even had a website address and flyers available. I doubt seriously the sponsoring agency knew anything about the interlude. At the conclusion of the program, the presenter again plugged the book.

All told, more than one-eighth of the seminar time was an ad for goods that had nothing to do with the topic in question.

 **TIP** Don't sell from the stage unless it's part of the program. If you have a sponsoring organization, be sure promoting your products is acceptable. Ending with product sales is only appropriate in a sales call.

SIN: Announcing the Ending

Pick your ending: *"And in conclusion..." "In summary..." "You can go ahead and put away your stuff, this is the last thing I'll have to say."* I'll bet these presenters never taught in a college classroom. In the college classroom, if you so much as hint that the end of class is near, the only sounds you hear the next few seconds are note-books slamming shut, laptop lids clicking closed, and bookbags zipping up.

 TIP Don't announce the ending. Let it be a surprise. If you do say *"This is the end,"* then you've got one sentence to finish because you said it was the end.

SIN: Providing No Clear Ending

You've heard this one before: *"Well, if there aren't any more questions, I guess that about wraps this up."* Or, *"That's all I've got."* And the worst: *"I had some more information for you, but we've run out of time."* OK, that isn't the worst. The worst is when the speaker says they've run out of time and still doesn't stop!

The end of a presentation should tie up the loose ends. If you made a promise, it's time to deliver. If you need to clarify roles and action items, now's the time. Quickly. It's time to stop.

TIP End as you started—use the method that got the audience's attention at the beginning to cement the main ideas into their minds at the end.

Summary: Content Should Be Remembered

How can we know that we have succeeded in the area of content? We look for two results from Content:

1. Our audience receives, accepts, and takes our message home, and
2. Our audience does the objectives we had for the communication—they respond to the call to action.

One is almost completely within the speaker's control; the other is not. But there are many ways to maximize the potential of both.

To develop effective core content:

1. Find Empathy,
2. Find the Essential, and
3. Make it Entertaining.

Empathy allows us to understand our audience. **Why** are we speaking to them? **Why** are they listening? **Who** are they? What are their characteristics? Based on the Why and the Who, what are the **Objectives** for this presentation? Finally, **What** is it we need to get across to the audience?

Understanding the **Essential** message of our presentation allows us to structure it in a flexible, reusable way. We can adapt it to different audiences and different timeframes.

A quick **Reality Check** will ensure that our essential message and structure is on the right path to reaching our audience. Are they receptive? Do we understand their expectations?

We need to choose a structure that will **Entertain** our audience, that is, hold their attention, so they will consider what we have to say and even adopt our ideas. Using the **Speaker Grid** makes it clear which pieces of content support which key points.

Finally we add our **Open Block**, which consists of getting our audience's attention, giving them a reason to listen, and removing obstacles, as well as a **Close Block**, where we summarize our essential message, make a call to action, and wrap up gracefully.

Now that's impressive.

CONNECTION:
Your Communication Relationship

Connection Made

The comedian takes the stage. He warms up the audience and gets a few chuckles. He picks up the pace and the volume of laughter increases. Then he hits them with the big guns and gets the guffaws, the belly laughs, the sustained laughter that requires him to pause until he can be heard again. Success.

The CFO kicks off the quarterly management meeting in the auditorium. As she talks through the numbers, the yawns cease, the attendees sit up in their seats, and some people even begin to take notes. When the Q&A arrives, the hands shoot up. And as the auditorium empties, the chatter about financial results continues. Ah, success.

The keynote speaker at the luncheon expects to start with half-attention from his audience. As he's introduced, the hum of chit-chat at the tables lowers but continues, along with the clinking of forks against dessert plates and rattling of ice cubes in nearly empty glasses. As he begins to speak, the chatter dies down. He continues, and people stop shuffling through their meeting materials; the whispers cease, the forks stop in mid-air. Every face is turned toward him. Ah, impressive success.

When a relationship is felt between the audience and the presenter, attention is high. There is a buzz in the room—or rapt silence. You'll find smiles, joy, and sometimes tears, but "it" is there. Some people call it engagement. Some call it interaction. It's been referred to as charm. It's been labeled charisma. Whatever it is, it enhances communication and makes an audience pay attention.

Let's take a look at the third element of the Three Cs model—we call it Connection.

The Importance of Connection

When the comedian or CFO or keynote speaker connects with the audience, it is not happenstance or coincidence. These occurrences can be predicted with some degree of certainty. The comedian uses examples that audience members think came directly from their living rooms. The CFO calls out different teams for congratulations on their performance, demonstrating how each one contributed to the overall business results. The keynote speaker speaks uses his voice to draw his listeners in as his story ebbs and flows with drama. The end result is the amazing "*He was talking to me!*" feeling that makes the hair on the back of a listener's neck stand up. Or the "*OMG, did you spy on us last night?*" reaction when the comedian imitates your bossy oldest child. In the world of business meetings, the feeling might be "*I know that manager has my best interest at heart.*"

Connection has a "something for everyone" feel about it, and a speaker who maintains that focus will be rewarded with his audience's attention and often an invitation to return.

In our context, "connection" means "link; bond" and "association; relationship." We are linking hearts and minds. We are creating associations in the minds of our audience and building a relationship with them. Because connection involves human emotion and

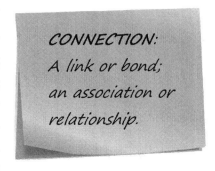

CONNECTION: A link or bond; an association or relationship.

psyche, it is not an exact science. People have different learning styles. Some prefer visuals; others would rather hear you talk. People have different senses of humor. Cultures vary greatly: across nations, companies, and municipal boundaries. Background, age, experience, attitude, and your reputation all have an effect on the connection you can create with your audience.

But without a connection...you won't have an audience for long. They'll be texting or sleeping.

Ways to Connect

While it may seem like some people are natural connectors, Connection is more than a personality type.

Several key elements contribute to the success of your connection:

- **Storytelling** – Entertaining your audience with relatable stories
- **Humor** – Interjecting humor (which is more than punny jokes)
- **Language** – Using clean, clear, understandable words
- **Interaction** – Involving the audience in the experience
- **Visuals** – Using effective visuals that support your message
- **Q&A** – Asking for questions and answering them effectively

Let's examine some of the connection techniques that cause us to sit up and take notice as well as the common problems with them.

Storytelling

Storytelling is one of the greatest connection methods of all time. Stories are part of every known culture at every stage of history. Stories are much more likely to be repeated than facts. Stories predate written communication, and I'll bet you can repeat the stories I've told in this book more than you can recall the definitions I've given (which is the primary reason I include stories).

When people ask for a secret to great presentations, one answer tops my list: the use of stories. I can just about guarantee that a presenter you love uses them. I can assure you that keynote speaker you want to hear uses them. I'll bet your favorite teachers tell stories frequently.

Stories are so effective at carrying a message that they were the vehicle for great communication before we invented writing. Stories are repeated across generations, persist long after a leadership change, get told and retold by multiple recipients, and still are able to carry the message even when the details get fuzzy. Stories can bridge cultural boundaries, generational gaps, and get even the most bored audience to perk up in seconds.

Stories are magical. Great presenters strive to use stories perhaps more than any other tool in their arsenal.

However, stories aren't so magical that you can use them indiscriminately. If all you aspire to do is tell stories, then you're missing the point (unless you are the story time leader at the library). You should definitely use stories, but use them well.

Storytelling Techniques

There are several techniques that enhance storytelling:
- Using **details** to create images
- Using **drama** to create interest
- Using **dialog** to create relatable characters
- Using **personal stories**
- Using **familiar stories** *with a twist*

Use Details to Create Images

Details are critically important to a listener. Consider the following two story snippets.

Story snippet 1: As a kid, I went to the hardware store a lot. I loved going there!

Story snippet 2: Before I was even old enough to go to school, my parents would let me walk the three blocks to Ray's Hardware. The store smelled like a cross between motor oil and freshly turned dirt. I couldn't even see over the counter, but I loved hearing Mr. Ray's raspy voice ask, *"Hey, kid, what'll it be today?"* Mr. Ray always gave me a Blow-Pop when I left the store. I'll never forget Mr. Ray and the love I had for his store.

What's the difference? It's the same story, but one of them creates a movie in your mind. When you picture it, you remember it. This is one of the reasons that stories are so powerful.

But details take time. You can't (ever) give all of them. Match your level of detail to your time and your objectives (which you should know before you start the story).

Use Drama to Create Interest

In the 1991 film *City Slickers*, Curly (Jack Palance) challenges Mitch (Billy Crystal) to discover the "one thing" that is most important in his life. The film develops the plot with the unresolved drama that Mitch has yet to discover his "one thing." This method of building tension is of course not unique to *City Slickers*. Most films have some element of unresolved conflict in them. It's what keeps the viewer tuned in and watching to the end.

Stories benefit from drama as well. Drama makes the listener lean forward and wonder about the outcome. In a business story, it could be as simple as wondering about the results of a marketing initiative. In training, it could be the awe of a new tip or trick (*What else can she show us?*). In a meeting or assembly, it could be the announcement of a special guest.

 TIP Create unfulfilled drama in your stories. Don't be in a hurry to reveal the answer. Let the audience want it.

Use Dialog to Create Relatable Characters

I asked a student to tell the class about a person who had influenced his life. The result exceeded my wildest expectations for this exercise. The student chose to talk about a high school coach that had changed his life trajectory and purpose. The story itself had great details, outlining a less-than-stellar playing career and a disappointing spell of riding the bench. The drama came to a head when the player confronted the coach to ask what he could do to earn time on the field. The conversation was classic.

"Coach. I think I have something to offer to the team. I've been busting my tail in practice. How can I get some playing time?"

"Son, you do have something to offer this team. I had planned to cut you in tryouts, but we had one spot left and I asked the AD who I should keep. When I gave him my list of names, he picked you. He said, 'That's your "glue" kid. He'll be a leader and keep all the others playing together. He probably won't help you on the field, but he'll be a great asset in the locker room.' I've watched you for the last few weeks, and he was right. You are an incredible leader. Others follow you. Everyone on our team needs to have a role. Williams is our rebounder. We count on

Baker to score. You're our inspiration and example of what hard work can do. Your time on the court may come, but know your true role."

The student went on to speak of how the coach's comments inspired him and how he applied the lesson to his life whenever he was down. He could have lectured on the subject himself. But by bringing in his former coach and the athletic director, he created characters the audience could relate to and thus voices of authority that the audience would want to listen to.

As an added bonus, with no coaching, he changed his voice inflection when quoting his coach, providing another interesting Conduit element to enhance the listening experience.

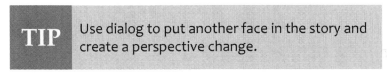

TIP Use dialog to put another face in the story and create a perspective change.

Use Personal Stories

The American sports industry focuses almost exclusively on the extrinsic results of sports: winning in order to get scholarships and eventually a pro contract. Yet the vast majority of the tens of millions of participants in America will never become pros. Only 3.4% of high school athletes play at the college level, and less than 2% of those will ever earn a dime playing their chosen sport. If you coach your whole life and see 1500 kids roll through your program, you'll be lucky to have one that ever goes pro.

I'm part of an initiative to educate and challenge youth sports coaches to not be win-at-all-costs tyrants but rather to encourage and influence these athletes' lives for the better. When addressing coaches in this program, there is merit to using an anecdote from Vince Lombardi, John Wooden, or Pat Summitt. But if I do that, there is a strong likelihood that my audience has already heard the story. They may listen politely but without the same attention they had the very first time they heard it.

Instead, I use personal stories. Since I've spent thousands of hours on the field, on the court, and in the locker room, I've got plenty of material. The principles and stories relate to any coach from the peewee leagues to the pros.

My sports anecdotes tend to be fairly straightforward. They contain emotion but don't drown the listener in it. Sometimes, though, we tell stories are full of deep, intense, personal emotion—losing a child, facing devastating illness, enduring physical hardship, going bankrupt, having loved ones betray you.

Death, loss, disappointment, and mistreatment all are elements of the human experience. Your story can have a profound impact on those who hear it when told with thought and intentionality. Your story puts the audience in your shoes, and allows them to reflect on their own similar experiences.

The first time you tell a difficult story, you may find yourself extremely emotional. Practice out loud in front of a real person before you attempt to share it with a larger audience.

Big or small, funny or emotional, your story is yours. For better or worse, it's what made you who you are. Your story can inspire me to face my own problems and challenges, and consider the change you are trying to create.

Use Familiar Stories with a Twist

I open one of my keynotes with a less-than-one-minute intro about the town of Gettysburg, Pennsylvania, and the event they scheduled for November 19, 1863. Most of the audience hears Gettysburg and makes an instant connection. (Side note: I don't use this story if the audience is largely international, because it won't connect as well.) I expound on the story and end up asking, *"Who did the leaders in Gettysburg ask to be their keynote speaker?"*

Occasionally (maybe one out of ten times I speak), I'll get the correct answer, but the far more common outcome is for people to shout out, *"Abraham Lincoln!"* I'll let a few answers go by and respond, *"That's right—Edward Everett!"* Then I finish the story.

People become *really* engaged when they realize they don't know what they thought they knew.

Storytelling Sins

SIN: Telling Stories without Purpose

A friend recommended I attend a presentation by a woman he described as a "fascinating speaker." She was coming to the local area and, with that kind of introduction, I quickly agreed.

The speaker was interesting and funny. She told a lot of good stories. Her energy was contagious. Everyone seemed to enjoy themselves.

But I cannot for the life of me recall what she said, because her stories did not lead to a larger message. They were just stories.

One of the most egregious sins a storyteller can commit is to take time (and frequently too much time) telling a story that doesn't have a point that fits the presentation. Sometimes this is identified blatantly (*"That doesn't have anything to do with what we're talking about today, but I thought you'd like it"*), and sometimes it is less obvious (and often called into question by the audience). Regardless, a great presenter will use stories to effectively make a larger point and not tell them just to pass the time.

 TIP Your presentation has an essential message. Make sure the stories you tell support that message.

SIN: Telling Stories with Too Many Details

A friend wanted to introduce me to another friend of his. He told me how he met the friend twenty years ago, what college the friend's son currently goes to, about a vacation they shared two summers ago, and about a medical condition his friend suffers. This was all to tell me that this friend has a business complementary to mine and we should meet for coffee.

For detailed-oriented folks, stories can digress into a hard-to-follow trail of details that may or may not be meaningful. (Phrases like *"Let's unpack that a little"* and *"Oh, that reminds me"* are indicators of speakers who see detail.)

 TIP Know how long your story should last, and match the detail level appropriately. Choose to share the details that give your story the most "oomph."

SIN: Telling Stories with Missing Details

We've seen that when telling stories, details make the audience picture the scene in their minds. It would seem any level of detail will do, depending on time. The audience will usually fill in any gaps with meaning. But some details can't—or shouldn't—be omitted.

One type of omission is failing to tell the audience the conclusion. If you've created drama, you need to resolve the story. Paul Harvey always gave *"the rest of the story."* If you fail to provide a return on your audience's emotional investment, expect to answer lots of questions after your presentation.

The second type of omission is when there is a jump in time or logic that leaves the audience wondering what happened. This is where the Curse of Knowledge lurks. You know all the minutiae. You probably don't realize that you missed a pertinent detail. But the audience needs to follow the story, and huge gaps leave them more confused than engaged.

The first time I ever used a story in class about how I met my wife, I managed to leave out some rather important details that left the audience confused (and surprised). *"It was 7:45 a.m. New Years' Eve. The doorbell rang. I opened the door and there she stood: the woman of my dreams, the one I would marry. There were slight complications, such as my current girlfriend standing behind me at the moment and the fact that this beauty and I wouldn't speak again for several more months."* While I thought I was being clever and creating drama, the audience just had lots of questions. When I started to move to the next topic, several in my class stopped and shouted out, *"Whoa! Finish the story! What was going on at 7:45 in the morning? Did you want to date her then? Why was she knocking on your door?"*

Omitting details that give critical information and context leaves your audience confused and wanting more. Wanting more is good; confused is not. Just because *you* know the story, don't assume the audience does. This is where a trial run before a live audience is helpful to work out the gaps in your story.

(P.S. My wife really did show up on my doorstep. She was joining a large group of college football fans on a trek to a bowl game. We had mutual friends, and the group's assembly point was my house. We both ended our relationships in the next few months, and the next time we met, our spark began as a business relationship—I bought graphing calculators from her for my calculus students.)

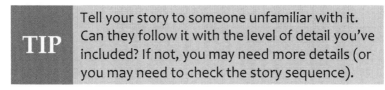

TIP — Tell your story to someone unfamiliar with it. Can they follow it with the level of detail you've included? If not, you may need more details (or you may need to check the story sequence).

SIN: Overlooking a Bombshell

"On my very first day of school, I walked past the body of my dead uncle on our porch on the way to class. The kindergarten teacher was named Miss Sally, and she was really nice. We all got our own crayons for drawing and mats for taking naps on the floor. And then..."

Wait—WHAT? I actually have no idea what the second sentence was—or the third or fourth; I was still busy processing the thought of a five-year-old seeing a dead relative and having to continue on like nothing was wrong. That's a big emotional barrier for an audience to overcome.

> **TIP** The most effective story-telling technique is the pause. When you drop a bombshell, let it sit. Move across the room. Show a visible facial expression. Let the audience know it's OK to have their own emotional reaction to the story.

SIN: Telling Common Stories

At the National Speakers Association convention many years ago, speaker after speaker made fun of the starfish story. You've likely heard it (if you haven't, Google it). The story ends, *"But I made a difference to that one."* I remember the first time I heard that story. It was touching; I was moved. The second time I heard it, I was polite. The third time, I ruined the punch line for my seatmate. After that, I just sighed and daydreamed. Kudos to author Loren Eiseley—it was a great story—the first time. It was popular enough to be used in a wide variety of forums. But when told to an adult audience that has heard it before, it loses its appeal.

> **TIP** When using a familiar story, making sure it has an unknown twist. Better yet, tell a personal story.

SIN: Getting Facts Wrong

One of my students was giving his final exam presentation. His slide and his voice announced, *"When the Space Shuttle* Challenger *exploded in 2003..."*

My mind went numb. I have no idea what the next few minutes were about. I was too busy doing two things: 1) reminiscing about one of the defining moments of my generation (made all the more poignant by the fact that I watched in person as the *Challenger* fell from the sky), and 2) looking for other facts that this presenter had missed. The *Challenger* exploded January 28, 1986.

When you make mistakes on basic facts, the audience may believe you, which means you're misleading them, or they may catch your mistake, which means you'll lose them.

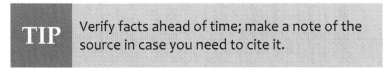

TIP Verify facts ahead of time; make a note of the source in case you need to cite it.

SIN: Not Telling Stories

I was coaching a technical expert for a national conference breakout session. He was a guru in his field, had a lot of cool material to share, and was terribly boring. At a dry run for his presentation, he lamented that the audience didn't seem very engaged, and he wanted to make a good impression on the larger stage that was coming up. I made note of the fact that he had talked only facts and technical content. I suggested a different approach.

I started with, "*Sum up your entire presentation in one sentence.*" Once we got to the crux of his message, we brainstormed a way to introduce the concept. Further questioning led to a story about his childhood relationship with his brother. Aha! I suggested he share the story as a way to introduce his topic with human interest and offer an easy analogy to drive the entire presentation.

When I explained where I was going with all this, he stopped me and said, "*I don't think anyone wants to hear about how I fought with my brother.*" I disagreed and asked him more questions about normal experiences for people with brothers. He conceded that he had lots of friends with similar experiences. As far as those who didn't, he acknowledged that they would understand and appreciate the humor even if it wasn't their own experience.

As he left, he told me he had doubts about the effectiveness of this approach, but he was willing to try it. He did, and when he came back, he was beaming. He said people stayed at his presentation for another thirty minutes, most of them connecting with his story, but then discussing the technical merits of his presentation.

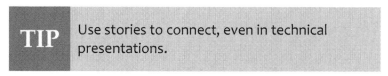

TIP Use stories to connect, even in technical presentations.

Humor

What makes a speaker interesting or fun? Humor—appropriate humor—comes in near the top of the list. We all enjoy a good laugh. Professors that can make us chuckle while taking notes about differential equations have their classes fill up while the monotone lecturer who wrote the book gets only overflow and transfer students during registration.

Humor is valuable to a presenter because it represents a huge connection. The audience was listening. They heard and understood what you said. And they had a positive emotional connection.

Humor Techniques

I took a workshop from a professional comedian who said a stand-up comic strives to create four laughs per minute. That's one every fifteen seconds! I've observed speakers for the last decade, and in the business world, speakers are considered funny if they average a laugh from their audience every two minutes. A funny business presentation has *one-eighth* the amount of humor as a comedian! (And that's nothing to laugh about.)

The overwhelming impression I got from this comedian was how *hard* comedians work at humor. They constantly seek out new material to try out on friends and small groups before risking it on stage. They script out virtually their entire show. (Improv is another story and requires a different skillset.)

I've had many people tell me, *"I'm not funny."* Usually they are right, but that doesn't mean they can't *become* funny. Here are three methods to start increasing the humor factor in your presentations:

1. **Observe** the world around you (journal!),
2. Build humor into your **storytelling,** and
3. **Poke fun** at yourself.

Look Around—The Human Condition Is Worth a Laugh

Probably the best tip for improving your humor is to start observing the world around you. Humor is what's funny about real life. It's the disconnects and mismatches. It's the odd juxtapositions. It's the irony of wishes granted. If you look at the rest of humanity and don't find some measure of humor, I'd suggest you might not be paying enough attention.

So pay attention. Write it down. There is your humor material.

Build Humor into Your Storytelling

Most stories, even serious ones, have elements of humor in them. In fact, heavy stories sometimes *need* humor, not only to offer contrast to the serious elements, but to lighten the emotional load for the audience—to give them a break. Watch how gifted storytellers work humor into their tales, then try it with your own stories.

Poke Fun at Yourself (Why not? Your kids do.)

Self-deprecating humor is usually safe within certain limits. Poke fun at yourself, but only if it shows a connection and common bond with your audience. I get a lot of mileage (for a few more years at least) from stories about my kids. It shows that 1) I'm not a world-class parent and 2) my kids are normal. I also laugh at all the dumb things I've done on stage and the lessons I've learned from them. (Heck, I've even written a book about them.)

Finally, if your humor succeeds, and the audience laughs, then let them. Smile. Pause. Let them laugh. When they're done, you can start again.

Humor Sins

At best, the sins of Humor get you groans. At worst, they get you fired. Use your comedy wisely.

SIN: Using Scripted Jokes (Orange You Glad I Didn't Say Banana?)

You're tasked with presenting the company vision at the quarterly management meeting and you open up with *"A German, a Frenchman, and an Italian walk into a bar..."* What emotion and reaction am I supposed to conjure up?

Jokes do not equal humor.

Plus, jokes are likely to have been heard before (especially in the Internet age), leaving audiences not knowing how to respond. (Laugh politely? Groan? Walk out?)

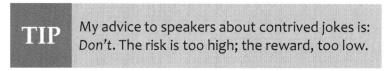

TIP My advice to speakers about contrived jokes is: Don't. The risk is too high; the reward, too low.

SIN: Using Off-Color Humor

I watched a white speaker in a predominantly white church open with a scripted joke with a punch line referring to someone known to everyone based upon news headlines, who happened to be African American. It doesn't matter how funny the joke was (it was marginal at best), it was inappropriate, reeked of unprofessionalism, and was probably offensive to many people in the audience.

Because I had a cursory knowledge of the speaker and was a young and learning speech coach, I reached out to him and asked what his intent was in delivering the "joke."

He said, "*I was a few lines in before I realized I was even telling the joke. I wanted to stop, but I had started and had to finish. I'm sorry I ever brought it up, but felt that changing midstream would bring even more attention to my mistake.*"

Ouch. He was trying to "forget" an issue, when he might have been better off "fixing" it. "*Hey, this is a stupid joke. I don't know what I was thinking. I'm sorry. Please forget I ever started it.*"

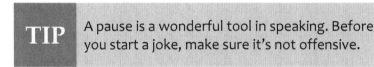

TIP A pause is a wonderful tool in speaking. Before you start a joke, make sure it's not offensive.

Language

When students challenge me that speaking well is an innate rather than learned behavior, I counter with, "*I've never known a human who was born speaking. We all had to learn it somewhere.*"

So many of our communication skills are cultural—most of the time we learned these skills (and sins) from others. Since that is the case, the proper use of language and development of our language skills is critical to the exchange of ideas.

Language Techniques

When it comes to the language we use for speaking, the same skills that make an effective writer make an effective speaker. Clear words. Precise thoughts. Concision. Active rather than passive language. Correct usage and grammar.

At the core, though, we want the audience to understand what we say. Longtime friends and family can communicate with a glance or a grunt. Business teams can frequently finish each other's thoughts. Often the wrong word or phrase is okay because the audience understood it completely.

The more common mistake is to misuse language because of a gap between the audience and the speaker. It's far too easy to use words and phrases that confuse an audience. This is an area in which we can all strive to improve.

Language Sins

SIN: Using Jargon

In my son's first year of tackle football, the coach kept calling a play in practice that was failing miserably. As a volunteer assistant, I suggested that perhaps we needed to explain to them what a "trap block" was. The coach's response was telling: *"We've been running the trap since the first week of practice. Of course they know what it is."* On the way home, I asked my son what a trap block was and how it differed from a normal block. He played a position (tight end) that was heavily involved in the play, and was part of the reason the play wasn't working. He started to respond, then sheepishly admitted he had no idea what a trap block was. Based on the performance, I'll bet he wasn't the only member of the line without that critical piece of knowledge.

Every industry, profession, hobby, and curriculum has them — words that are unique to that industry, profession, hobby, or curriculum. A basic step to improvement in any field is understanding the terminology so you can talk with the experts, teachers, and coaches. In our classes at MillsWyck Communications, we explain what we mean by "spray," "stop," "low shrug," "go big," and "the TCP." Otherwise, our coaching efforts would not be effective enough to change behavior.

When presenting a topic with many unfamiliar words, one of my favorite techniques is to use a glossary, only I don't fill in the definitions. Instead, I ask the audience to write in *their* definitions and explain what they think the words mean, just like I did with the trap block.

If you're not getting results from your team, you might first investigate their knowledge of the words you use. Language has a huge influence on learning.

 TIP Simplify everything. Evaluate the words you use from the audience's perspective with a critical eye. Don't assume they know what you mean.

SIN: Using Words You Don't Know

As a graduate student, I had to make a presentation in a math class. I opened by stating the theorem I had been asked to explain. "*Let $f(x)$ be a homomorphic function…*" Before I even finished my first sentence, the professor interrupted, "*Mr. Hoffler, do you know what* homomorphic *means?*" The word was usually in the first sentence of every theorem I had studied for two years. I had become quite comfortable with its presence. I recall that I once questioned what it meant, but I didn't major in math at the undergraduate level. No one else ever seemed to pay the definition any mind, and gradually I lost all interest in knowing what homomorphic meant. It was acceptable to everyone, so it was acceptable to me.

Now on the spot and on the hook for a definition, I could only go to root word analysis. Well, homo = same; morph = shape.

"*Same shape?*" It doesn't make any more sense to me now than it did to me then, but I was scrambling. My professor smelled blood, and we both knew it. He pounced. "*Class, Mr. Hoffler is about to explain to us a theorem about a function which he doesn't know how to define. Can one of you please explain to him what a homomorphic function is?"* I expected everyone to shame me with quick explanations but was surprised when there was silence. Their faces indicated I wasn't the only one ignoring the word's meaning. The professor was almost giddy. He attacked them as well, for which I was temporarily relieved. *"You mean to tell me not one of you can explain what a homomorphic function is?"* No one could.

He then explained that a homomorphic function was something that was so well-behaved that it lacked all useful application. He claimed that nothing in the real world would be modeled with such a function. It was used to simplify matters for analysis and theory. His parting shot and smug face is something I'll never forget: *"Mr. Hoffler is going to explore this theorem about a function that is useless for explaining anything that really matters. Please continue."*

By the way, I did get an 'A' in the class, and it was one of the hardest and most fun classes I had in graduate school.

TIP If you use a word, make sure you know the meaning of it. (Incidentally, presenters should know the difference between the *podium*, what you stand on, and the *lectern*, the stand that holds your notes.)

SIN: Speaking in Generalities Rather than Specifics

It seems the higher one is promoted, the less specific one becomes in communication. That's partly to be understood—an organizational chart shows that people near the bottom have the most specific details and the most granular tasks. The C-level is about the big picture. But too often, the C-suite converts clear communication into a stream of buzzword bingo. You're more likely to hear *"We need to leverage our domain strategy to empower our customers and stabilize our market growth with win-wins based on our value proposition"* than *"If we give our customers an unexpected surprise during our brief transaction with them, they'll do backflips to buy more and they'll even tell others about us. Go find ways you can amaze our customers."*

The more abstract your message, the less you really have a message. *"The development team needs to share their code changes with the testing team before they build them"* is a lot clearer than *"We need our project leads within the development function to collaborate on their strategic initiatives."*

Action follows understanding which follows clarity of message.

> **TIP** Always choose the specific over the generic. It is more connective, and it eliminates confusion and apathy.

SIN: Repeating Words

As we got up from the dinner table one night, an unusual conversation started a most humbling experience for me. My son (age ten) told me, *"Dad, you say that a lot."*

Me: *"Say what?"*

"'Sitting around scratching my head, thinkin'.'"

"That's ridiculous, son. I don't ever say that."

"You just did."

"Really?"

"Yes."

Having learned that you don't argue with a ten-year-old's observations (they're always right, just ask them), I responded, *"Well, maybe. But it's probably the only time. That's crazy."*

We went about our business. Thirty minutes later, while dog-sitting for a neighbor, I was engaging the Missus in conversation while the kids tended to the pup. I may have been as shocked as anyone to hear, *"I was just sitting around, scratching my head, thinkin'..."* My son sprinted into the room, vindicated, yelling, *"SEE! I told you that you said that."* Daggone it. He was right. That once.

Then over the weekend, I said it *three more times*. He caught all three. On the last one he just smiled. The next week I said it twice in class—once *after* I had told this story. What a crazy phrase! Who says that? Me, apparently. A LOT.

Shortly thereafter I had a phone conversation with a colleague who teaches presentation skills classes as well. Usually I talk to him in person. After a few minutes on the phone, I noticed he said *"You know"* quite a bit. I started counting. In the following twenty-five minutes, he uncorked that phrase ninety-one times! That's one "you know" about every fifteen seconds.

I watched a person giving a seminar on speaking say the word "team" 169 times in one session. He was a professional, lauded for his prowess on the stage.

We all have our demons. And our "word."

 TIP You might not know what your word or phrase is, so you may need help to find it. Ask your significant other, a colleague, a ten-year-old, or Mr. Canon what your word is.

SIN: Using Foul Language

A person I knew only slightly asked if I understood his business model. When I said no, he launched into an explanation of it. Fifteen minutes later, I had a good idea of how he controlled his business and also was pretty convinced he had no control over his mouth. He uttered no fewer than twenty expletives in those few minutes. Many had no meaning or function in a sentence. (The Internet reports that the F-bomb can function as all nine parts of speech. That doesn't mean you should allow it to.)

Before you label me a prude, it's worth saying that I grew up around enough sports that foul language rarely bothers me. The issue isn't what offends *me*; it's what offends *your audience*. Even more simply, does your language prevent your audience from listening clearly to what you have to say?

If your response is, *"I don't give a <bleep> what they think,"* then I might refer you to the opening chapter of the book where we talked about mindset and Rule #1. You can say whatever you want; you can't choose your audience's response. So unless you're onstage as a vulgar comedian and the audience is lit, my advice is to keep your colorful phrases to a G or PG rating.

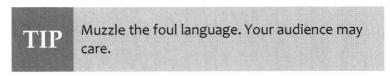

TIP Muzzle the foul language. Your audience may care.

SIN: Missing Double Meanings

I was leading a very interactive group through a presentation workshop. One of the participants asked about personality types and their implication on communication. I immediately thought of a colleague who lectures solely on this topic and knew that I did not have the expertise to address the question correctly. Here's how I answered the question: *"There are tools to help you with that. I am not that tool."*

It was several minutes before everyone was able to regain a straight face.

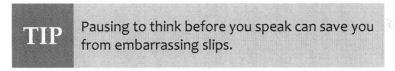

TIP Pausing to think before you speak can save you from embarrassing slips.

SIN: Separating Yourself from Your Audience

A local college football coach was a passionate, fire-breathing, inspirational leader who had lofty dreams of championships. The alumni at the university were thrilled with his vision and attitude. After several years of results far below the championship promised, the grumblings began. With the pressure came a noted change in the post-game interviews. The coach put distance between himself and the press as well as between himself and the fans.

The most damning phrase he used was *"You people."* It started occurring with such frequency that the local paper picked up on it, blogs were filled with references to it, and people began to mock it.

Be careful of the pronouns you use when referring to the audience. If they are "you" and you are "me," then you aren't one of them. The collective "we" is a solution that works often. (Of course, if you're telling a first-person story, it's always "I.")

 TIP Seek to find commonality with your audience rather than highlight differences. Use language that connects rather than separates.

Interaction

Malcolm Knowles revolutionized the theories of adult learning and how they differ from those for educating children. One of his theorems is that adults like to bring their life experiences and knowledge to learning. They don't enjoy a lecture as much as a conversation. I've found this to be true in practice. Audiences want to be involved. An engaged audience learns better; plus, it's more fun.

Interaction Techniques

My time as a corporate trainer gave me many professional development opportunities to learn about interactive training techniques. These methods can be used in almost any environment: meetings, webinars, sales calls, and presentations. Unfortunately, very few communicators take the time to learn them, and even fewer practice enough to become skilled at using them.

Bookshelves are full of ways to transfer information other than by lecture. Consider using discussions (whole group and small group), role plays, exercises, brainstorms, case studies, videos, interviews, quizzes, and e-learning, reading and review (don't discount this as a learning strategy; most of your college education came this way). Even games can be used to liven up your delivery and get the audience to repeat the essential message they need to receive.

Interaction Sins

SIN: Ignoring Your Audience

I walked in to a full-day corporate training class to find the instructor sitting behind a computer. Perhaps he was making final adjustments to the course slides; perhaps he was troubleshooting a network connection; perhaps he was instant-messaging his mom or playing Angry Birds. I don't know. I do know that he didn't even raise his head to acknowledge me or the other students arriving. Would you be surprised if I told you the class didn't improve from there?

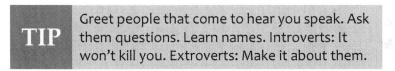

TIP Greet people that come to hear you speak. Ask them questions. Learn names. Introverts: It won't kill you. Extroverts: Make it about them.

SIN: All Lecture, No Interaction

At a seminar for trainers (who frequently make the worst audiences for training events), the presenter went through a half day with virtually no interactive elements. The audience asked questions several times and even tried to participate, but the presenter soldiered on. Apparently she needed to reach the end of the program in a specified way. Once, she even said, *"I have a lot of material to get through, and I can't finish if you keep interrupting me."* (Recognize a Rule #1 violation, anybody?)

By the end of the half day, the audience had a look of resignation, knowing that they would not be able to participate in their own learning except to listen to the (boring) speaker.

> While a lecture is a valid way to present, consider some other options. In most settings, interaction will keep your audience better engaged. They want to participate. Really.

SIN: Defaulting to the "TCP"

A student of mine had completed our multi-day class on creating training programs. He went back to his office to apply what he learned. He came back with a three-hour seminar that consisted of nothing but PowerPoint slides, ordered and delivered as the Typical Corporate Presentation. I asked him about the other methods we had discussed in class. *"I considered them, but I think PowerPoint will work the best."* I couldn't have disagreed more. The reviews from his seminar confirmed my belief. His "TCP" was dreadfully boring.

> PowerPoint has its place, but on its own becomes dull. Mix things up a bit. Add games, group discussion—*something* different!

SIN: Calling on Individuals without "Permission"

Attending a boring webinar, I did what most people do: I started reading and responding to email. I was shocked out of my electronic stupor with the sound of my name called by the moderator. She then asked, *"What do you think?"* Since I had no idea what it was I was supposed to be thinking about, my snarky response would have fit in with my son's elementary school classroom more than it did a professional webinar. It was unprofessional, and I immediately regretted it.

I've been on the other side of the question too many times to recall. I've found that calling on people who have not volunteered or raised their hand to indicate interest will most often work contrary to your expectations.

In the education world there are mixed views about calling on individuals. Even those in favor of making on-the-spot queries with a name attached will advocate that you ask the question of everyone before putting an individual pupil on the hot seat. Engage everyone. Let everyone ponder the answer. Embarrass no one. Rule #1 is at work here.

In my classes, I never use a name with a question unless there is insider knowledge. If I have a participant who has been a math teacher, I don't mind saying to her, *"Margaret, I know you know this. Tell our class the definition of a continuous function."* The last time I did this (yes, I find a way to use continuous functions when I'm speech coaching!), her face lit up. She asked back, *"Do you want the delta/epsilon definition or the graph definition?"* I smiled, and we both enjoyed the moment knowing the other people in the room thought we were positively crazy.

 TIP Don't randomly call on someone to participate unless they indicate interest or the application is directly related to them and what they know.

Visuals

No tool or invention has done more to shape the world of presentations than PowerPoint. According to the source of all knowledge (Wikipedia), PowerPoint is used somewhere in the world 350 times *every second*. The original software, bought by Microsoft in 1987, was designed to make visuals more precise, impactful, and easier to produce. With all its bells and whistles to attract the attention of geeky users, our culture quickly adopted the tool as a way to fulfill several needs: notes to remind the presenter what to say, handouts to give the attendees, and a visual to watch during the presentation. Rarely, if ever, can you do all three well with one entity.

But PowerPoint is not the problem. Presenters used overblown content and data-dense visuals long before computers were invented. Viewgraphs, foils, chalkboards, and overheads were used for decades, and the same mistakes (sins) that presenters used in the 1950s migrated forward as the millennium came to a close. PowerPoint only made it easier to sin. (Now you also can toss in Apple's Keynote, Prezi, open source Impress, and so on.)

There is probably no area of communication that contains more sins that Visuals. Most of my coaching clients who ask for help with their "presentation" mean that they want a slide makeover. They've seen a good presenter work seamlessly with visuals and want to mimic what they've seen. But what they don't realize is that visuals are a subset of a class of skills—visuals are one way to CONNECT. Visuals are not the presentation. Visuals should *enhance* the presentation. A great presenter should be effective with NO visuals.

General Guidelines for Visuals

Visuals are important. Set aside time to complete them well (or better yet, hire a professional to do them!), but do them last (see the Content chapter). Slides should be done when you are sure of what you're going to say, not as you are figuring out what to say.

Reasons for a Visual

Once you have your message complete, you can use two questions to help you design visuals for any particular point in your content.

1. What's the point I'm trying to make?

2. How can I make that point more effectively with a visual?

Many points can be made without a visual. Stories make points very well and frequently don't need a visual to be effective. However, if you're expected to create visuals or think they would be useful, here are five reasons you should probably use a slide:

1. When the audience absolutely MUST get the point.

2. When it's easier (or quicker) to make the point with a visual. If I'm talking about the size of Texas, an overlay may make the point much better than describing the area with facts. A picture often is worth a thousand words.

3. To make a point from data. Don't show the data, necessarily, but the chart, trend, or conclusion the data creates.

4. To show progress. If you have three points, you might show that you finished point two and are moving to point three.

5. To create emotion, including humor. When I tell personal stories, I often use pictures to go along with them, which not only verifies the story as true, but helps emphasize the funny aspects.

I'm sure there are other acceptable reasons (one of them might be that you are required to use them, although I personally dislike that reason a great deal), but until someone proves there is another category, stick with these five.

Guidelines for PowerPoint Slides

Many presenters try to type every bit of their content into PowerPoint. If you don't know what point you're trying to make, typing in content so you won't forget it may sound like a good plan, but it's not effective communication and won't be appreciated by your audience.

When creating slides, use these strategies:
- One major point per slide
- Limit the content
- Make it easy to read

Failure to follow these guidelines will be apparent as we go through some Visuals Sins.

Visuals Other than PowerPoint

Just because it's the most accepted tool in the presentation world, don't assume that PowerPoint is the only way to use visuals. Props and objects are sometimes more effective, especially for smaller crowds. Information guru Edward Tufte brings a real copy of Euclid's *Geometry* (a book published in 1570!) to his presentations. Seeing the physical book makes his point a lot more than a picture or a description on a slide.

Visuals Sins

Perhaps the greatest sin you can commit when it comes to visuals is the belief that your visuals *are* your presentation. Since beliefs govern our actions, putting slides ahead of content means your focus and energy are on your visuals and not your core message or what your audience needs. No audience needs more or prettier visuals. Their true needs are around their business, their thoughts, their problems, and their ability to affect the world.

SIN: Reading the Visual

The number one complaint about PowerPoint presentations and training classes is *"The speaker read to us."*

The temptation to read from slides can be avoided by not putting anything on your slides that's readable. If you can't read it, you won't read it.

Look at the slide labeled "Capabilities," taken from a technical sales presentation deck.

Capabilities

- Design flexibility on PCB and switch design. From 2 to 64 output combinations from up to 6 output lines are possible.
- Higher number of outputs for more precise control of features like water levels and temperature management.
- Binary, Gray Code and custom coding available.
- Switch life of 100K cycles at load is typical.
- Cam operated butt contacts (AC or DC)
- Push-to-turn and push-to-set switch options available.
- PCB mounting and individual switch PCB designs possible.
- Plated contacts and PCB traces for longer life and accurate signal transmission.
- Full prototyping available.
- Design capability for custom actuator knobs available.
- No agency approvals, typically.
- Value-add opportunities!

Even though I have no idea what the slide is about or what the details mean, I could probably present it at least as well as the expert engineer, who would likely read it word-for-word (or close). Better yet, I could let the audience read it.

 TIP Eliminate readable text from your slides and you won't be tempted to read them to your audience.

SIN: More Than One Idea Per Slide

Why use gray code over a simple binary code? Why, indeed? Inquiring minds want to know.

Why Use Gray Code Over a Simple Binary Code?

A Gray Code is a modified version of the simple binary code.

With a Gray code, the binary outputs change by only one bit each time the numeric numbers change at each increment.

This helps to eliminate the possibility of false output signals because there is no way of guaranteeing that all the bits will change simultaneously at the boundary between two encoded values.

Example: If straight binary were used, it would be possible to generate an output of 15 (1111) in going from 7 (0111) to 8 (1000).

This slide actually has several points. The first section is a definition of gray code. The second tells how gray code works. The third tells the benefit of using gray code (and thus answers the question). The fourth section offers an example. All on one slide.

That should be four slides, not one. Four points. Four slides.

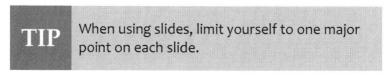

TIP When using slides, limit yourself to one major point on each slide.

SIN: Displaying Too Much Data

It's a great temptation. You've got all this space. You've got all this data. Why not put the data in the space? One problem: it doesn't work for the audience.

Consider the following slide. Without knowing exactly what the point is, you already know it has problems.

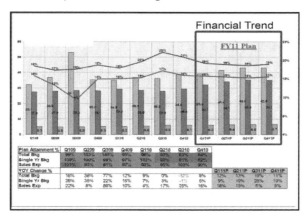

This finance update (Aha, *that's* what it is!) has bar charts. It has line graphs. It has numbers galore and tables with percentages. It shows quarter-to-quarter changes and offers a stoplight (red-yellow-green) assessment as well as a highlighted fiscal year plan.

It's virtually unreadable. You'd need a Controller or CFO to explain it (maybe that was the point).

At its core, though, I am hard-pressed to understand if it's good news or bad news. Am I going to get fired, or will I get a raise?

If you display graphs like this, be prepared to answer lots of questions or endure the sound of snoring.

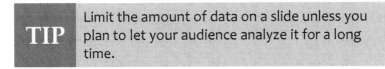

TIP Limit the amount of data on a slide unless you plan to let your audience analyze it for a long time.

SIN: Showing Content that Isn't Readable

I watched an executive give his "roadshow" presentation to his staff—over 400 people—live in an auditorium. He handled the presentation the same way he did with clients: by drawing the concepts on a whiteboard.

It's worth interjecting that drawing on a white board is not a bad idea—the drawing process can actually engage the audience's mind. But an approach that works sitting with three people in a board room is much more difficult to pull off with 400 people in a theater setting. The whiteboard idea might have worked if the board had been projected so everyone could see it. It was not. Additionally, the whiteboard was not clean, the executive's handwriting was miniscule, and his marker was nearly dried out. The result was a disengaged audience that wondered why the speaker mumbled with his back to them while he scribbled illegible material.

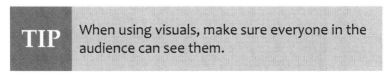

TIP When using visuals, make sure everyone in the audience can see them.

SIN: Complex, Detailed Diagrams

I sat through a presentation about one of the many reorganizations at a former employer. As expected, a new organizational chart was displayed to share the details of the reorg.

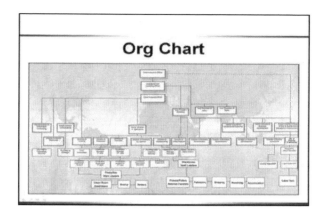

Of course, the slide was so detailed, no one could read it. As a result, no one could follow what the presenter was saying. Well, at least we all knew there were people in the organization.

> **TIP** Your visuals should be readable by every member of your audience. If you need to share a complex diagram such as an org chart or system diagram, it is better to share it as a handout (in a font large enough to read).

SIN: Asking a Question without Providing an Answer

Here's a slide from a leading cancer researcher.

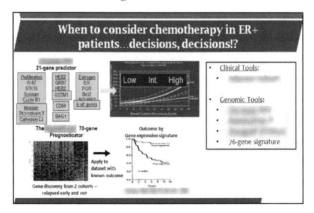

He asks an important question: when should you consider chemotherapy in your cancer treatment? If I had cancer, it's probably one of the top questions I'd want answered.

But nowhere on the slide can you find the answer. This physician may be the only person in the world who could interpret the data on this slide. I'd want the point to be *"Never!"* or *"Always!"* or even *"It depends..."* (with whatever it depends on clear as a bell).

> When asking a question on a slide, your audience should be able to find the answer on the slide without your help.

SIN: Using Your Slides as Your Handouts

I took a three-day class on a very technical subject matter. If three days weren't daunting enough, we walked in the classroom to see a five-inch thick binder full of content at each desk. When the trainer started walking us through the book and we realized that every page was a carbon copy of the slides that were being displayed, it became excruciating.

When you have a handout ready for attendees as they show up, the first thing they do is thumb through it. When the handouts *are* the content/visual/presentation, there is no surprise. There is no suspense. There is no reason to listen. They might make up their mind that *"It gets interesting at slide 96,"* but that actually disengages the audience because they've presupposed there is nothing between now and then that demands their attention.

Plus, when you use your slides as handouts, you almost always have too much information on them.

Take the example here (1st Day Preparation "Warm Up"). It is slide 1 of 4, delineating what appears to be the onboarding process for a new employee.

1st Day Preparation "Warm Up"

1. **Task: Plan Work** – Conduct an analysis of the current jobs; current "checkbook" and schedule status; and who is working the jobs;
   - Warm Up Event: Works with Coach to "catch the bubble", develops Work Plan, develop "Hot Jobs" List
   - Supporting Tasks: Understand Work Packages, Network with Key Players, Technically Competent
   - 1st Day Event: Issue Job Assignment for each mechanic at Start Up

2. **Task: Lead by Example** – Conduct 1st Day Start up Briefing with Crew; communicate personal style, establish ground rules, and goals.
   - Warm Up Event: Prepares first day speech and rehearses it with the Coach.
   - Supporting Tasks: Live the Values of the Company; Demonstrate Ownership of Work (Quality), Understand Union Contract, Gives Clear Direction to Subordinates.
   - 1st Day Event: Give 10 minute Start Up Briefing to entire crew.

3. **Task: Job Assignment (Match Jobs to People)** – Conduct 1 on 1 assignment sessions with every mechanic on crew
   - Warm Up Event: Coach creates "role playing scenario" with own crew and rehearses/observes 1 on 1 session and provides feedback.
   - Supporting Tasks: Crew Development and Performance and Set Expectations and Provide Feedback (Pulls available personnel data and personal background information on entire crew prior to first day.)
   - 1st Day Event: Interact 1 on 1 with every mechanic on crew during first day to Assign Jobs, Set Expectations and Provide Feedback.

There is simply too much to take in. This slide most likely was intended as a handout. Had the presenter asked, *"What's the best way to show this visually?"* there never would have been such a slide.

> **TIP** Your handouts and slides serve different purposes. Slides should enhance your talking points. Handouts should provide more detail for future reference and should be designed to help take notes or reinforce the message.

SIN: Not Proofreading

Spell-check is wonderful. While I'm old enough to remember life before spell-check, I have no desire to go back. It helps. But human check is better than spell-check.

At my former place of employment, a major corporation, the head of security sent an email to the entire company offering the opportunity to buy shirts at an event in order to support a wonderful nonprofit. Only he forgot a single letter. In the word *shirt*. With a sentence structure that made the misspelling quite comical.

At his retirement he was given a shirt commemorating the event, and he rarely presented where people didn't shout out questions about shirts. A simple proofread would have saved a world of embarrassment.

 All ways get an other sit of Ides on you're slider, you're memes, you're marketing maternals, and you're e-snails.

Q&A

Answering questions well drives a high connection with an audience. The audience gets their needs met while the speaker appears to care.

But answering questions might be THE hardest area in which a communicator can excel. You don't know what they're going to ask (or do you?). You don't know what you should say (or do you?). You have to manage an entire audience, but are dealing with the stated needs of only one member of the group.

It's hard. But following the process below helps make it manageable and beneficial for your message and your image.

Q&A: Use Your EAR

Managing questions is easier when we break it up into steps. There are four, with the notable exception that step one might be skipped if your audience jumps right to it.

1. Ask for questions

Once the question is on the floor, we will use the EAR method to get in and out of the process: Empathize, Answer, Return.

2. Empathize: Acknowledge the question

3. Answer: Respond to the question

4. Return: Exit the question and get back to your message

Ask for Questions

Speakers often want the audience to respond or interact. This is good; an involved audience is an engaged audience, thus more likely to retain what is being discussed.

The poster child for a poor question request is in the movie *Ferris Bueller's Day Off*. The teacher (played by Ben Stein) was a poor Conduit by using a monotone voice, and his technique in asking for questions was terrible as well.

"Anyone? Anyone? Raised or lowered? Did it work? Anyone? Anyone know the effects? Anyone know what this is? Class? Anyone?"

Only slightly better is the question, *"Does anyone have any questions?"* The problem with this query is that the answer is either Yes or No. If someone does ask a question, technically she isn't answering what you asked. Plus, that query (*Does anyone have any questions?*) seems to assume that there are no questions, since it asks whether they exist.

A better way to get questions is to make them welcome and assume they are present in the minds of your audience members. We also want to encourage audience participation. We do this through the Magic Word of Questions. What is the magic word? you ask. That's right. "What" is the magic word. Just by opening your questions with the word "What"(or sometimes "How"), you make them far more interesting and engaging. Try using *"I know this is new, and there must be questions on your mind. What questions do you have for me?"* or *"How else can I help?"*

Empathy: Acknowledge the Question

You've been told that there is no such thing as a stupid question. Whoever postulated that theorem clearly never taught high school. Or was a corporate trainer. Or led a meeting. Or interacted with humans on a regular basis. Sometimes, there are very stupid questions, and you still have to answer them.

One of the main difficulties with questions is that the questioner has an advantage over you, the speaker. They know what is about to be asked (well, most of the time!). You do not.

To acknowledge the question (good, bad, or otherwise):

1. **Listen** – Don't interrupt the questioner before she finishes asking the question.

2. **Empathize** – If the question has a noted emotion behind it, connect with the emotion. *"I understand how you could be confused"* or *"This appears to be an important question to you."*

3. **Summarize or paraphrase** – Restate the question (without parroting) to confirm understanding. This can be particularly important when the questioner rambles or isn't quite sure what he is asking.

The purpose of empathy is to assure the questioner that his needs are being met. Connect with any emotion (*We all want the business to grow…*). Make a broad statement that he can agree with (*Everyone wants to attend the conference in Hawaii*).

Radio financial-show host Dave Ramsey is a master of answering questions with empathy. A caller will phone in: *"I make $25k per year. My truck cost $60k and I just had someone run into me without insurance. I found out my insurance had lapsed. Then my air conditioner at home went out and my dog has cancer. What should I do?"*

The easy answer for a financial advisor would be *"What the heck are you doing with a $60k truck?!"* But Mr. Ramsey will say something like, *"Wow. It sounds like life has been using you for a punching bag. That sounds hard. You must really feel low."* He connects before he tells them what to do (stop spending money you don't have and find a better job).

Answer: Respond to the Question

At the core of answering questions is the answer. A poor answer is like a speech without good content. You can use whatever template you want, but if you don't answer the question, the audience is left wanting more.

The basic rule of thumb: Answer the question in the least amount of time possible in the manner the audience member wants. If a technical person asks, she probably wants a technical answer. An executive wants the summary. A client of a CPA wants the steps to follow.

If you don't know the answer, the best tactic is to admit that fact (*"I don't know."*). Your next phrase should be, *"But I'll find out."* Of course, this assumes the answer exists and you will go find it.

Return: Exit the Question

Once you've given your best answer (or deferred the answer to later), it's time to regain control and move to the next question or get back to your presentation content. This is where many speakers lose their credibility. Perhaps the worst phrase you can utter at this point is, *"Did I answer your question?"* Many times you can know the answer to this binary question (see the problem already?) with a glance at the questioner's face. Asking if you answered the question is inviting trouble. If you did answer, great. You were supposed to. If you didn't...uh oh. You gave your best answer, and it wasn't good enough. There's a disconnect somewhere, and that's exactly what you were trying to avoid by asking for and answering questions in the first place.

The technique that works the best is to use the question as a springboard to get back to your core message. We call this a "return."

Think of your Speaker Grid. (Remember it from the Content chapter?) If the question is even remotely connected to what you've been talking about, you've got a great opportunity to review a key point. The question you were scared of thirty seconds ago is now a perfect chance to reiterate what you want the audience to know.

For example, I frequently get rather contentious questions about how fake it feels to use the Energy skills, and the mere thought of "acting" is repulsive (especially to the more knowledge-based workers like us engineers). These questions get phrased more as indictments, as though I am a huckster trying to create a Billy Mays schlepping product and win people over. (I promise I have nothing against Billy Mays. He was a great communicator, but our purposes are very different.) I've had some students who won't let it rest.

Look at how I can use these contentious questions as a reinforcement for two things I want the audience to repeat: Rule #1 and Rule #2. Note how I open with empathy…

"You're right. It doesn't feel natural for most people, including me. That's why it's so hard and why you aren't already doing it. What I'd encourage you to focus on is the execution of just one of the skills. Maybe gestures or a vocal variation. Work on that one skill. You'll be surprised at the changes you can make with a small amount of effort. But please do try. This brings us back to a great reminder of our foundational rules. Rule #2 says that the way we feel is different from what the audience feels. So all I ask you to do is find out if the audience thinks it's crazy before you decide not to do it, and if you truly believe Rule #1 (it's about the audience, not you), then you'll do what they ask."

I've given the question validity, told the questioner and the rest of the audience members what they need to do, and then I've come back to a principle that I wanted to reinforce anyway. All in a few sentences. The EAR method works!

Q&A and the Conduit

Because the Content aspect of answering questions can be stressful, it's easy to forget that our Conduit is still driving impressions and is a huge part of making a Connection with the audience. The proper behavior to exhibit when taking and answering questions comes from our Control skills (poise, pause, and eye contact), which drive the audience's impression that we are confident. Focusing on Control skills may be hard because of the Gap—we probably feel anything *but* confident as we answer difficult questions.

Physically, make sure you exhibit neutral posture when taking questions. Smile at the questioner. Take steps towards him, if appropriate. Do not cross your arms or back away. Drop your arms and act like you want to be there. (You *love* taking questions!)

When answering the question, demonstrate Empathy to the questioner. Give the specific Answer directly to the questioner, but offer any further explanation to the broader audience (in other words, make eye contact with the questioner first, then with all of the audience). The Return (your exit from the question) should encompass all audience members. When it's time to exit, do not stand near the person who asked the question. Instead, move away from that person, make eye contact with someone else, and ask for the next question or return to your material.

Showing Control (even when you don't feel it) in a difficult Q&A tells the audience that you are professional and confident, unfazed by the "attack" you are enduring. Your solid behavior gives credibility to the answers you are crafting with the EAR method and provides a springboard to regain control of your presentation.

Q&A Sins

SIN: Offering to Take Questions without Waiting for Them

A nationally known speaker in his field hosted a webinar with hundreds of people on it. About halfway through, he made the comment, *"Well, it looks like we're ahead of schedule a little bit. How about I take a few questions. Moderator, please put the phones in conference mode. Any questions? ... Well, it looks like I must be explaining things pretty well then. Moderator, put the phones back in presenter mode."* And off he went. The pause represented by the ellipsis? Less than two seconds. I know—I counted.

Consider what has to happen for me to ask a question. I need to formulate my understanding of the topic. I have to identify where I missed understanding or what the issue is. I need to craft the question in words. Finally I have to decide if I have enough nerve to ask my question on a national call. And the presenter gave me...two seconds. That's not enough time to accomplish the mental exercises necessary to ask a question.

 TIP If you ask for questions, pause longer than you think you need to (and a pause means you are not talking).

SIN: Asking Too Many Rhetorical Questions

The speaker cranks out a rhetorical question, something along the lines of, *"Have you ever wondered the purpose of rhetorical questions?"* But before you, the listener, can consider the question, the speaker continues, forging ahead on the path he wants to follow regardless of whether you are following along. His question is just a stepping stone to his answer, not an indication of interest in your possible answer.

While questions can be a very powerful tool to connect with your audience, when the audience senses that their use is merely a construct to help the speaker talk, they backfire. Again, go watch the Ben Stein *Ferris Bueller* clip on YouTube for a horrible (and horribly funny) example of how to present information.

 Use rhetorical questions sparingly. When you do use them, make them thought-provoking, allow a pause for the audience to consider the answer, THEN continue.

SIN: Asking Questions without Waiting for Answers

I watched a presenter give a ten-minute informative presentation about a topic of interest to everyone in the audience and in which he was a bona fide expert. In the course of those 600 seconds, he asked his audience no fewer than twenty-four questions. He didn't wait for a single verbal response. In fact, there was not so much as a pregnant pause after any of the questions.

It quickly became obvious that asking questions was not a way to engage the audience but rather a long way to start a sentence so the presenter could think about what was coming next. A quick glance at the audience also revealed a side effect: virtually no one was listening attentively.

This is a frequent characteristic of speakers who promise in the opening that they are going to be interactive. They shout out a few questions, they get a few responses, and then they gradually (or suddenly) stop waiting on audience responses and answer their questions themselves.

The audience picks up on the speaker's intent pretty quickly. They realize the speaker doesn't intend to engage them but is using questions as a setup to give information.

 Use questions as a setup sparingly. Otherwise they lose meaning (and the audience loses interest).

SIN: Undermining Empathy with "But..."

There is one word that cancels whatever attempt you are making for empathy: "But." It negates any emotion that precedes it. *"Honey, I love you. You are so beautiful,* but..." We're through if I utter those words. ("However" will get you similar results.)

> During the empathy stage of questions, don't utter "but" or "however." Instead, try "and" or simply insert a pause.

SIN: Qualifying the Question

An audience member asks a question. Before answering the question, you try to create empathy by saying *"That's a good question."* Except...you've undermined the empathy attempt by qualifying the question.

When you say *"That's a good question,"* the implication is *"Your last question wasn't good!"* When you say *"I'm glad you asked that,"* the implication is *"I was unhappy with the other questions."* And note the pronoun used: *"I'm* glad." Remember Rule #1.

Instead of focusing on the question, we want to connect with the questioner. And while we don't want to judge the question, we do want to clarify it (especially if it was long or covered multiple points). To accomplish both these tasks, begin with *"I heard you ask..."* This approach focuses on the questioner ("I heard you") and helps make sure that you are on the right path before you begin answering.

> Use non-qualifying phrases to connect with your audience during Q&A. *"I heard you ask..."* and its variants are a good start.

SIN: Answering Too Long

A professor of mine, known for dry lectures, got excited in class one day. It all started with an innocent question: *"Hey, how does <random topic> fit into what we've been studying?"* The answer should have taken two minutes. Instead, the professor become visibly excited (we found out later it was his research area of expertise). He took all fifty minutes of the lecture to answer, thereby putting our semester schedule behind by one class period. While the lecture was fascinating, we were less than happy when the next test included material that had barely been covered in class.

TIP Answer questions concisely--in line with the depth of the question. Do not sacrifice the essential for the interesting.

SIN: Making Up Answers

In my senior design project in engineering school, a classmate was doing his part of our final presentation before a slightly bored and somewhat testy faculty committee (as well as a roomful of classmates/peers). At one point, a very pertinent question arose from a senior faculty member: *"Where did you get that coefficient?"*

Since the project was dealing with something that had never been done (and still hasn't), the coefficient was not an empirical fact that we could reference. Furthermore, we lacked the research facilities (not to mention know-how) to accurately reproduce an environment where we could find out. All the literature had different numbers because of different assumptions with predictably different results. We were hoping against hope this question wouldn't come up, but it did.

Looking back, I suppose a truthful answer would have been *"We made it up."* Given the implications to our pending graduation, that probably would not have been an acceptable answer. Today I'd probably suggest taking the tack, *"Since this has not been experimentally replicated, we can't know for sure, but the existing research and leading minds seem to adopt a number between 0.4 and 0.5. Our research confirms the results with these acceptable parameters."*

Instead, my friend gained a reputation that day with his response: *"From the Walldorf paper. It's an accepted value."* What made that a particularly gutsy move was the fact that Walldorf was sitting a few rows behind the questioner that day. He never said a word.

 TIP Don't make up answers when solid evidence or data is available. To support statements that facts cannot prove, reference expert opinion and your personal experience.

SIN: Saving Questions until the End

I was at a conference where a speaker concluded his talk and opened the floor for questions. *"That's all I've got. I'll take questions now."* After a pause, a hand went up. The question became a long-winded diatribe, which sparked a few other responses. Two questions became twenty. Five minutes became fifteen. But here's the kicker: only about five people in the audience were involved. The rest of us were ready to go (judging from body language) after "That's all I've got." When the argument hit ten minutes, people began to leave. Many stayed, not sure of the protocol and not having been released to leave. I stayed until the next breakout session needed the room, and the discussion resumed in the hallway. Those of us not engaged in the questions were never acknowledged, and most of us were reading the conference brochure.

Q&A can engage an audience, but done poorly, it can lose one as well.

 TIP Save your ending ("the Close") until after Q&A. Put a time limit on the Q&A, and make yourself available after the talk for additional questions.

Summary: Connection Drives Interest

If you are presenting to robots, then emotion is not necessary. If your subordinates always do what you say, no matter what, then persuasion is not required. If your students are all perfect and take notes on everything you present, then you can jump right in and give them the facts.

For the rest of us who are speaking to humans with short attention spans, a million other tasks vying for their attention, a bit of skepticism, and a whole lot of forgetfulness, connecting with their minds and emotions is necessary. We must connect to get our audience to listen and become involved with our message.

Storytelling is one of the most powerful ways to connect, whether you tell your own story or a familiar story with a twist. Use details, drama, and dialog to create image, interest, and perspective.

Humor is a wonderful part of the sometimes-puzzling human condition. Use it wisely, but definitely use it.

Use **language** that is clear, concise, and targeted for your specific audience.

Adult learners in particular need more than lecture—they need **interaction**. Look for ways to create some back-and-forth with your audience.

Visuals are not just a way to present Content; they are a way to create Connection. Be sure to understand your message first; *then* create visuals to support it.

When handling **Questions**, use your EAR: Empathize with the questioner, Answer the question, and Return to your message or move on to the next question.

Use your Connection skills to create a bond with your audience. When you link with hearts and minds, a relationship is forged that garners a high level of interest from the audience.

CONCLUSION

Bringing the Cs Together

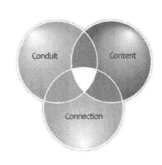

In virtually any area of life, it is rare for one person to be naturally capable in every needed skill. An athlete might be fast but struggle with hand-eye coordination. A business leader might be incredibly talented at seeing strategy and planning tactics but lack people skills. Our friend may be caring and able to comfort us but lack the skill of punctuality.

It is no different with communication. I've met people who were gifted at crafting speeches and putting together training programs but couldn't (or wouldn't) deliver the training in a manner that would keep anyone awake. One of our students realized that he had made a living working his natural skills of Connection (which is why he'd made a name for himself in sales) but had never developed the skills of the Conduit and lacked Content most of the time.

Where then should you start? The answer is simple: it's less important *where* you start than that you *do* start. Pick a skill. Pick a method. Pick a tip. But get better. Don't assume or hope that it will happen naturally. Many of the Sins we've seen in this book came from well-intentioned but poorly trained presenters.

As we discovered in our opening chapter, all the presenters we admire have a journey of development. They want to get better. They got training. They practiced. They developed their skill and ability. They learned to stop sinning and start impressing.

My Presentation Journey

I haven't always held the views in this book. In fact, I was one of the biggest offenders of Presentation Sin(s), and I didn't even know it.

Even though I'll be quick to point out that I'm not perfect, I have the video to prove that I am significantly changed from that high school math teacher a quarter a century ago. That change is what makes me believe that anyone can become great as a presenter.

Everyone's journey is unique, but maybe some of the tools that helped me on the path to improvement will help you too. Here are three of the most important ones:

- Journaling observations
- Recording and reviewing yourself
- Hanging out with great speakers

Journal Observations

In athletics, a player who wants to excel will frequently do all she can to learn, practice, and soak up the environment. Golf enthusiasts hang out at the clubhouse, watch the Golf Channel, subscribe to *Golf Weekly*, and dream about golf. Pilots go to the airport to watch planes land, listen to air traffic control in their spare time, and will do anything possible to get time in the cockpit. Any cockpit.

Put another way, these people become "students of the game." If you want to be a great speaker, adopt this mentality. Learn everything you can about presenting.

For me, this concept manifested itself through journaling. As I started to learn and improve my presentation skills, I never watched a speaker without a pad and pen in my hands. My journal was simple. I drew a line down the middle of the page and wrote headings at the top:

This works	This doesn't work

I'd put down every observation of the speaker into one column or the other. I'd catalog them when I got home and write a blog about a particular aspect that impressed me. This served two purposes. First, it made me acutely aware of what good speakers do. Second, it honed my skills of observation. I began to see traits that I had never noticed or cared about before. As I began to notice the skills in others, I became far more critical of myself. That's when I began to see marked improvement. It started with a journal.

Record and Review

Most of us don't like to see or hear ourselves in recorded form (*What? Do I really sound like THAT?!*). But for speakers who want to improve, it's a must. I met a man who told me he had hundreds of his presentations recorded. *"But I never listen to them."* What a waste! If you have the recordings, use them! Learn from them!

My favorite speech coach is Mr. Canon. His siblings Ms. Nikon, Miss Panasonic, Mr. Sony, and Mrs. Samsung are equally as capable. Even first cousins Mr. iPhone and Mrs. Galaxy will do the trick. Just record yourself. Then watch it.

Even if you've already had feedback from a peer review (such as a workshop audience) and a speech coach, there are three things that sink in when you review a recording of yourself:

1. The tone of your voice
2. The pace of your speech
3. The motion of your body

Oh! I know you said I needed to stop waving my arms—NOW I get it!

I find video to be the most critical resource a speaker can utilize, but embrace any recording of yourself, audio or video. Whenever possible, record yourself. Use video in practice. Use audio on the phone.

Then chisel out time to listen and watch (as difficult as it may be!). Compare the recordings to what you want to become as a speaker.

Even short recordings can be beneficial. For example, I use my commute times for audio review. I can set the phone up to record myself through my car microphone. I'll tell a story, then play it back, then tell it again. I can do a three-minute story several times during an errand run.

Hang Out with Great Speakers

I realized early on that I can learn something from any speaker. Sometimes it is because they have a sin I notice (blog and book material!). But almost always, speakers use skills or execute their stories in a way that is better than I would have done it. By noting and trying to emulate those who are better than I am, I stretch my abilities and make myself better.

I attend a speaker club that meets once a week, not as a speaking coach, but as a speaker in search of improvement. I want to get better, and being around people who are better than I am is a great way to do it.

The Final Sin: A Fixed Mindset

There's one more Sin before we depart.

These pages are filled with observations and tips on how you can be a more effective presenter—how you can stop offending and start impressing your audience. I'd love to report to you that I'm perfect and do everything I've listed here. I'd like to say that all my students are cured from ever committing any of the sins we discussed, but presenting is a constant battle, an opportunity for growth.

That's one of the reasons I love the craft—the challenge to get better. The opportunity to affect others and to see their lives changed in positive ways keeps me taking notes, recording myself, and working with others to make them—and me—better.

You can be good, even great, with your skills. You can have all the content in the world, organized and suited to the audience at hand. You can connect and be a people-person extraordinaire. There is one more requirement to become a polished, world-class presenter: a growth mindset.

In her excellent book *Mindset*, Carol Dweck outlines two major outlooks that determine human achievement and behavior:

- **Fixed** – A fixed mindset says that talent is born, that you have all you are going to have.
- **Growth** – A growth mindset says that talent is developed. It sees possibilities and focuses on the process of getting better.

Alex Vermeer summarizes the mindsets perfectly: *"Having a fixed mindset creates an urgency to prove yourself over and over—criticism is seen as an attack on your character, and to be avoided. Having a growth mindset encourages learning and effort. If you truly believe you can improve at something, you will be much more driven to learn and practice. Criticism is seen as valuable feedback and openly embraced. The hallmark of the growth mindset is the passion for sticking with it,* especially *when things are* not *going well."*

Time and again, I've seen fixed and growth mindsets at odds in our workshops. One fellow argued for two full days about my coaching him to be more expressive. His practice videos showed he could execute the skills. His peers told him the results were fantastic, but he regressed back to his old habits every time a new practice session began. The class pleaded with him and told him how much more effective he was with the new skills. He told them it wouldn't work. We gave him feedback on what his audience wanted. He declined to even try, giving us a sad story about how his dad had lived a duplicate life full of lies and how *"That just isn't me."* He seemed to want to avoid showing any behavior that wasn't his "natural" self. His mindset precluded him from improving his behavior because the behavior wasn't "natural."

Contrast his story with Gina, a student who started our two-day presentation skills workshop with fear and trepidation. Her soft voice and halting manner of speaking had everyone dismissing her skill as a presenter. We were all shocked on the second day when she showed up and was using almost all the skills we were trying to teach. It was the most amazing overnight turnaround I've ever seen in our workshops. I had to find out why. Gina explained, *"I was so upset with my performance yesterday that I went home and practiced. I worked on the skills you told us about—pausing and eye contact. I spent three hours working on them in my mirror."* (By the way, Zig Ziglar practiced for two hours every night before he spoke, and he had done it for years.)

These two students were from the same organization! It's your choice which mindset to take. I know what I would encourage you to do: Be open to growth opportunities and embrace criticism. It's all part of being the best you can be, whether becoming a better parent, improving your basketball game, or learning new presentation skills.

Communication matters. At the core of our society and relationships is the exchange of ideas. I'm convinced we can all learn and grow in order to change the world around us for the better. I'm here to help do that in my circle of influence—and I'm cheering you on to excel in your arena as well.

Join me. Together we can rid the world of sinful presentations.

APPENDIX A: RESOURCES

What now? You've read the book, and know what to do. What else could spur you along the way or shorten your journey? Here are some suggestions to continue learning and practicing.

Resources from MillsWyck Communications

MillsWyck Communications' **website** (www.millswyck.com) offers free resources (blog, videos, newsletter) as well as information about our training and coaching options.

MillsWyck offers both public and private **workshops**, which typically range from half day to two full days. Private workshops can be customized to your organization's needs.

Individual **coaching** packages are available to help you shape your message, polish your presentation, and prepare you for the big stage. A diagnostic will help determine which package is right for you.

One of the resources you'll find on our website is the "What Not To Say" **video series**. These short (~3 minutes) videos poke fun at some of the crazy phrases speakers say. Because you've read this book, you'll immediately know why the phrases don't work. (http://www.millswyck.com/speaking-resources/videos/)

Alan Hoffler on Twitter:

www.twitter.com/alanhoffler

MillsWyck Communications' Website:

www.millswyck.com

MillsWyck Communications' Blog:

www.millswyck.com/blog

Free download: "Twelve Tips that Will Save You from Making a Bad Presentation"

http://tinyurl.com/q3u8v43

Frequently Asked Questions

Who's your favorite speaker?

While I certainly have my favorites, I don't like to tell people who they are for two reasons. First and foremost, my favorites are liked because they resonated with *me*. They connected with me. They may not connect with you.

Second, almost every speaker has some flaw or place she can improve (I certainly do). If you watch someone I say I like and she happens to have a flaw that is a pet peeve of yours, you'll think I'm crazy.

Instead of focusing on a few great speakers, I prefer to wonder what the perfect speaker would be like. Take the best of the best and roll them all into one. We can learn by watching most anyone.

Some names that students frequently bring up in our classes:

- Barack Obama – His posture and voice inflections are amazing.
- Bill Clinton – Always has a story to connect with regular folks, and his Arkansas accent doesn't hurt.
- Carly Fiorina – The former HP executive shows poise even in the line of fire.
- Joel Osteen – He practices twenty hours a week for a 30-minute message.
- Andy Andrews – The man can tell a story.
- Steve Jobs – Worked for three weeks to script a 30-minute presentation—and always had good news.
- Ellen DeGeneres – She always finds a way to connect. Maybe it's her goofy smile and ready laugh.

Where can I find good speakers to study?

The number one place I send people to watch great speakers is www.ted.com. Most of the speeches are short (eighteen minutes or less) and the topics are fascinating. (Sir Ken Robinson is a popular choice here.) WARNING: You can get sucked in and find yourself watching for several hours.

What about Toastmasters?

Toastmasters International is the largest public speaking organization in the world. I've been a member for many years. Here some pros and cons of Toastmasters...

Pros:

- Toastmasters offers an opportunity to be on stage. If you don't have many options to present regularly, I highly recommend that you join.
- Toastmasters offers great encouragement. Your club members will cheer and clap for you no matter what. It's the most enthusiastic audience you can find.

Cons:

- Toastmasters offers basic instruction ("use vocal variety," "use gestures," "organize your information," and so on), but the specificity can be minimal.
- In most clubs, critique of your presentation skills tends to be very gentle. And by "gentle," I mean "not particularly helpful." A frequent problem is that no one wants to hurt the speaker's feelings.
- Achievement of Toastmasters certifications, such as "Competent Communicator," requires only completion of speeches, not mastery of skills.
- Some Toastmasters clubs focus more on meeting protocol than on improving speaking skills. This tends to happen in

large, national organization where meeting structures are prescribed.

If you want to join Toastmasters, here's my advice:

- Shop around. All clubs are not created equal. Visit several clubs to see which one will offer the most helpful experience with your presentation skills (i.e., critical, objective feedback). Also make sure the club's a good fit for time and location, and that you like the people.
- Get professional presentation training prior to joining Toastmasters. Learn good skills and turn them into good habits by practicing.

Can I make money at speaking?

Probably. Many people make speaking their sole source of income. While I do make part of my living through speaking and advise many of my clients on the professional side of speaking, speaking as a business is more about marketing than it is about speaking. Yes, you have to be able to stand on stage and give coherent thoughts in a professional manner. Many of the tips in this book will put you well on your way to skills that can be sold. But ultimately you need to answer these two questions to have a future in the speaking business:

1. What do you have to say that is of interest?
2. Who will pay you to say it?

If you intend to make a career of speaking, the worldwide standard and source of networking is the National Speakers' Association (www.nsaspeaker.org). They are about the *business* of speaking, much more so than the craft of speaking.

How much can I make?

It varies. Bill Clinton frequently makes more than a half million dollars to speak for an hour. But I have tons of friends who would be thrilled to make $250 to speak. If you intend to speak for pay, expect that you will not make a livable income unless you are a known celebrity, an expert in your field, or a master marketer (or all three).

How long does it take to master these skills?

Master? A lifetime. But you can be amazingly good and better than almost anyone else you will see in just a few days...IF you practice the right things on a regular basis. Take the attitude of "always on" and use any opportunity to speak as a chance to get better. You'll be amazed at what you can accomplish!

Reading List

"You'll be the same in five years as you are today, except for the people you meet and the books you read."

—Charlie Jones, motivational speaker

Communications/Presenting

Atkinson, Cliff. *Beyond Bullet Points: Using Microsoft Office PowerPoint 2007 to Create Presentations That Inform, Motivate, and Inspire.* Redmond, WA: Microsoft Press, 2007.

Decker, Bert. *You've Got to Be Believed to Be Heard, Updated Edition: The Complete Book of Speaking . . . in Business and in Life!.* New York: St. Martin's Press, 2008.

Fugere, Brian, Chelsea Hardaway, and Jon Warshawsky. *Why Business People Speak Like Idiots: A Bullfighter's Guide.* New York City: Free Press, 2005.

Gallo, Carmine. *The Presentation Secrets of Steve Jobs: How to Be Insanely Great in Front of Any Audience.* New York, NY: McGraw-Hill Education, 2009.

Heath, Chip, and Dan Heath. *Made to Stick: Why Some Ideas Survive and Others Die.* New York: Random House, 2007.

Humes, James C.. *Speak Like Churchill, Stand Like Lincoln: 21 Powerful Secrets of History's Greatest Speakers.* New York: Three Rivers Press, 2002.

Morgan, Nick. *Give Your Speech, Change the World: How to Move Your Audience to Action.* New York: Harvard Business School Press, 2005.

Stolovitch, Harold. *Telling Ain't Training.* Alexandria: ASTD, 2002.

Weissman, Jerry. *In the Line of Fire: How to Handle Tough Questions... When It Counts.* Upper Saddle River, NJ: Pearson FT Press, 2013.

Weissman, Jerry. *Presenting to Win: The Art of Telling Your Story*. Alexandria, VA: Prentice Hall, 2006.

Creating Visuals

Altman, Rick. *Why Most PowerPoint Presentations Suck*. New York: Harvest Books, 2007.

Duarte, Nancy. *slide:ology: The Art and Science of Creating Great Presentations*. Sebastopol: O'Reilly Media, Inc., 2008.

Kosslyn, Stephen M.. *Clear and to the Point: 8 Psychological Principles for Compelling PowerPoint Presentations*. New York: Oxford University Press, USA, 2007.

Medina, John. *Brain Rules: 12 Principles for Surviving and Thriving at Work, Home, and School (Book & DVD)*. Chicago: Pear Press, 2008.

Paradi, Dave. *The Visual Slide Revolution: Transforming Overloaded Text Slides into Persuasive Presentations*. Mississauga, Ontario: Communications Skills, 2008.

Reynolds, Garr. *Presentation Zen: Simple Ideas on Presentation Design and Delivery (Voices That Matter)*. Berkeley, CA: New Riders Press, 2008.

Roam, Dan. *The Back of the Napkin: Solving Problems and Selling Ideas with Pictures*. Ottawa: Portfolio Hardcover, 2008.

Tufte, Edward R. *Envisioning Information*. Cheshire, CT: Graphics Press, 1990.

Business/Success

Carnegie, Dale. *How to Win Friends & Influence People*. New York: Pocket, 1998.

Collins, Jim. *Good to Great: Why Some Companies Make the Leap... and Others Don't*. London: Collins, 2002.

Collins, Jim. *How The Mighty Fall: And Why Some Companies Never Give In*. New York: Harperbusiness, 2009.

Dubner, Stephen J., and Steven D. Levitt. *Freakonomics [Revised and Expanded]: A Rogue Economist Explores the Hidden Side of Everything*. New York: William Morrow, 2006.

Dweck, Carol S. *Mindset*. London: Robinson, 2012.

Gladwell, Malcolm. *The Tipping Point: How Little Things Can Make a Big Difference*. New York: Back Bay Books, 2002.

Gladwell, Malcolm. *Blink: The Power of Thinking Without Thinking*. New York: Back Bay Books, 2007.

Godin, Seth. *The Dip: A Little Book That Teaches You When to Quit (and When to Stick)*. Ottawa: Portfolio Hardcover, 2007.

Heath, Chip, and Dan Heath. *Switch: How to Change Things When Change Is Hard*. New York: Broadway Business, 2010.

Lemov, Doug, and Erica Woolway. *Practice Perfect: 42 rules for getting better at getting better*. San Francisco, Jossey-Bass, 2012.

Maxwell, John C. *21 Irrefutable Laws of Leadership*. Waco, TX: Thomas Nelson, 2008.

Pressfield, Scott. *The War of Art*. New York, NY: Hachette Book Group USA, 2002.

APPENDIX B:
CHAPTER NOTES AND REFERENCES

Introduction
- Definitions throughout the book come from dictionary.com.

Foundation
- The phrase "Content is king" is believed to have been coined by Bill Gates in 1996. More information at http://www.craigbailey.net/content-is-king-by-bill-gates/.

Conduit
- Covey, Stephen M. R. *The SPEED of Trust: The One Thing That Changes Everything*. New York, NY: Free Press, 2006.
- For more information about English Language Learners, pauses, and thought groups, see http://www.elementalenglish.com/pausing-thought-groups-english-pronunciation/.
- The 2007 iPhone product launch with Steve Jobs and Stan Sigman can be found at http://thenextweb.com/apple/2015/09/09/genius-annotated-with-genius/. Sigman shows up around 1:08:30.
- Dr. Albert Mehrabian, known for his work on verbal/nonverbal communication, is currently Professor Emeritus of Psychology at UCLA. Visit his faculty page here: https://www.psych.ucla.edu/faculty/page/mehrab.
- It might be debatable how quickly first impressions are made, but it certainly is fast. See this article "How Many Seconds to a First Impression?" by Eric Wargo. http://www.psychologicalscience.org/index.php/publications/observer/2006/july-06/how-many-seconds-to-a-first-impression.html

Content

- German psychologist Hermann Ebbinghaus lived from 1850 to 1909. Wikipedia is a good starting place to read about him and his work: https://en.wikipedia.org/wiki/Hermann_Ebbinghaus.
- Morgan, Nick. *Give Your Speech, Change the World: How to Move Your Audience to Action.* New York: Harvard Business School Press, 2005.
- Heath, Chip, and Dan Heath. *Made to Stick: Why Some Ideas Survive and Others Die.* New York: Random House, 2007.
- Jim Valvano's ESPY speech can be found at http://www.jimmyv.org/about-us/remembering-jim/jimmy-v-espy-awards-speech/
- The full text of John F. Kennedy's 1961 speech can be found at http://www.space.com/11772-president-kennedy-historic-speech-moon-space.html.

Connection

- Sports statistics can be found at http://www.ncaa.org/about/resources/research/estimated-probability-competing-college-athletics.
- Malcolm Knowles was an American academic (1913-1997) who researched and wrote extensively on adult learning. He directed adult education at the YMCA and taught at Boston University and North Carolina State University.
- PowerPoint statistics from Wikipedia, September 8, 2015 (https://en.wikipedia.org/wiki/Microsoft_PowerPoint).
- If you haven't seen *Ferris Bueller's Day Off*, it's worth a watch just to see Ben Stein play the teacher. More info at http://www.imdb.com/title/tt0091042/.
- Learn more about radio financial host Dave Ramsey at http://www.daveramsey.com/.

Conclusion

- Dweck, Carol S. *Mindset.* London: Robinson, 2012.
- Read Alex Vermeer's summary of Carol Dweck's *Mindset* at http://alexvermeer.com/why-your-mindset-important/.

APPENDIX C:
DETAILED TABLE OF CONTENTS

ABOUT THE AUTHOR

 Raised around America's Space Program, Alan Hoffler has earned degrees in aerospace engineering and applied mathematics. Midway into his twenty-five years of training technical corporate audiences, instructing in the college classroom, teaching public high school, and speaking nationally to pilots about flying safety, he became fascinated with presentation excellence—how to achieve it and how to teach it. He believes that communication has the power to change a person, an organization, a community, and the world. With a coach's passion, a teacher's heart, and an engineer's mind, his writing reveals his desire to improve himself as well as his clients. When he's not speaking or training, he stays active serving in the local chapter of his professional organization, supporting activities and instructing in his local church, coaching and speaking about youth sports, and dreaming about using his commercial pilot's license. He is the co-author of *6 Steps Forward*, a parable about the stages in a man's life, and author of *Presentation Sin*, a collection of speaking tips he has learned as a speaker, observer, and speaking coach. His most challenging training endeavor is also his most enjoyable—raising two children with his wife Haley.

59914937R00115

Made in the USA
Charleston, SC
16 August 2016